ENTREPRENEURIAL TRAITS AMONG COMMERCE STUDENTS

ENTREPRENEURIAL TRAITS AMONG COMMERCE STUDENTS

By

Dr. Ismail Thamarasseri
Associate Professor
School of Distance & Online Education
Mahatma Gandhi University
Kottayam, Kerala, India, Pin - 686560

&

Ms. Parvathy Madhusoodhanan
M.Ed. Student (2021-23 Batch)
School of Pedagogical Sciences
Mahatma Gandhi University
Kottayam, Kerala, India, Pin - 686560

Published by:

DISCOVERY PUBLISHING HOUSE
4383/4B, Ansari Road, Darya Ganj
New Delhi-110 002 (India)
Phone : +91-11-23279245; 23253475; 43596065
Mobile : +91 9811179893 / +91 9871656464
E-mail : discoverybooksindia@gmail.com
orderdphbooks@gmail.com
namitwasan9@gmail.com
web : www.discoverypublishinggroup.com

Entrepreneurial Traits among Commerce Students
Authors: **Dr. Ismail Thamarasseri; Ms. Parvathy Madhusoodhanan**

International Standard Book Number: **978-93-6224-557-1** (Hardback)

Printed at:
Infinity Imaging Systems
Delhi (INDIA)

Preface

As the landscape of the Indian economy undergoes dynamic shifts, it invariably influences the educational paradigm. Education serves as the catalyst for cultivating motivation, self-sufficiency, creativity, and innovation – attributes crucial for navigating a successful career. In this context, our focus turns to the realm of commerce education and the imperative need to analyse the entrepreneurial traits among B. Com students.

The alarming prevalence of unemployment and underemployment among educated youth in our country demands a proactive approach. This book delves into the potential solution – channelling the energy and intellect of commerce students towards entrepreneurship. By providing proper entrepreneurial training and guidance, we aim to transform them into contributors to the economic development of our nation.

The educational landscape has evolved, with universities now incorporating entrepreneurship education to foster an entrepreneurial mindset among students. This book explores the nuances of entrepreneurial traits among B. Com students, recognizing that such skills are essential for the economic growth and development of a nation.

Drawing inspiration from global trends, we acknowledge the significance of entrepreneurship courses in universities worldwide. The narrative unfolds against the backdrop of India's rich natural resources, a burgeoning young population, and the persistent challenge of underdevelopment. It is underscored that for a nation to prosper economically, it requires entrepreneurs with vision, ambition, and the will to transform the economic landscape.

The Government of India has also taken steps to enhance entrepreneurial attitudes among the youth, implementing various schemes and programs. This includes integrating entrepreneurship education at the undergraduate level, a strategy aimed at fostering an entrepreneurial culture among students.

This book, titled *"Entrepreneurial Traits Among Commerce Students,"* emerges as a comprehensive exploration into the entrepreneurial landscape of B.Com students. It addresses the multifaceted aspects of entrepreneurial traits, aiming to uncover their levels, components, and variations based on gender, type of institution, and locality.

The methodology employed in this study utilizes a normative survey method, with a sample of 200 B. Com students selected through simple random sampling. The assessment scale, "Entrepreneurial Trait Assessment Scale," developed by Madhusoodhanan & Thamarasseri (2022), serves as the tool for analysing the entrepreneurial traits, spanning dimensions such as conceptual, technical, human relations, communication, decision-making, managerial, time management, stress management, personality and individual aspects, pioneering/risk-taking, unification and organization, and computer knowledge.

This book not only presents the findings but also highlights the broader implications for educational policymakers, administrators, teachers, and parents. It provides valuable insights for those committed to generating employment opportunities and encourages a re-evaluation of teaching methods to nurture entrepreneurial traits among students.

As we journey through the pages of "*Entrepreneurial Traits Among Commerce Students*," may it serve as a guiding light for educators, students, and policymakers alike, propelling us toward a future where entrepreneurial spirit flourishes, contributing to the economic vibrancy of our nation.

The authors express their sincere gratitude to all faculty members and administrative staff of School of Pedagogical Sciences, Mahatma Gandhi University for their valuable support and facilities given during the course of the study. The authors are grateful to their friends and colleagues for their emotional support and valuable ideas, which greatly helped in the completion of the study. In preparation of this book the authors had to refer to the works of other authors and information sources. The authors extremely indebted to various authors, editors, educationists, students and scholars whose views and opinions are integrated in this book. The authors shall ever remain obliged to their parents, teachers, friends, and family members for their kind guidance and assistance. Above all, the authors humbly solicit the God Almighty's blessings and is always thankful for the strength and presence of mind showered up on them for completing the work successfully. To them all, the authors offer their grateful thanks to M/s Discovery Publishing House, New Delhi who came forward willingly undertakes the publishing of this book.

Dr. Ismail Thamarasseri
Ms. Parvathy Madhusoodhanan

Contents

Preface

1. **Introduction** **1-47**

Theoretical Overview of the Study
Need and Significance of the Study
Statement of the Problem
Operational Definition of Key Terms
Objectives of the Study
Hypotheses of the Study
Methodology in of the Study
Scope of the Study
Limitations of the Study
Organisation of the Report

2. **Review of the Related Literature** **48-72**

Introduction
Discussion and Conclusion

3. **Methodology** **73-88**

Introduction
Objectives of the Study
Hypotheses of the Study
Method Adopted for the Study
Design of the Study
Population, Sample and Sampling Procedure
Description of Tools and Techniques Adopted
Statistical Techniques used for the Study

4. **Analysis and Interpretation of Data** **89-100**

Introduction
Entrepreneurial Traits Among B.Com Students

Entrepreneurial Traits Among B.Com Students based on its Components
Entrepreneurial Traits Among B.Com Students on the Basis of Gender
Entrepreneurial Traits Among B.Com Students on the Basis of Type of Institution
Entrepreneurial Traits Among B.Com Students on the Basis of Locality

5. Findings, Suggestions and Conclusion **101-107**

Introduction
Study in Retrospect
Methodology in Brief
Conclusion Based on Findings of the Study
Tenability of Hypothesis
Educational Implications
Recommendations of the Study
Suggestions for Further Study
Conclusion

Appendices **109-116**

Appendix 1: Personal Information Schedule
Appendix 2: Entrepreneurial Trait Assessment Scale (Draft)
Appendix 3: Entrepreneurial Trait Assessment Scale (Final)

Bibliography **117-125**

Index **127-130**

1

Introduction

"Education is not the amount of information that is put in your mind and runs riot there undigested all your life. The use of higher education is to find out how to solve the problems of life"

–Swami Vivekananda

Education is the greatest tool that always bring changes in the economy. It is the Golden key to open the doors of opportunity and prosperity. The universal declaration of human right adopted by the United Nation general assembly in December 1948 guaranteed the individuals a whole range of basic freedom with education serving as basic right necessary for the achievement of all other freedom. The fundamental principle of present-day education is that every learner should be given as much education or training he wants at a particular time. Instead of complete preparation for a life occupation, it may be just enough when an individual is equipped sufficiently with the knowledge and skill which may help him in meeting his immediate social or economic needs and responsibilities. The system of education should be designed in such a way that,it should prepare a person for meeting Occupational college and responsibilities under the rapidly changing socio-economic order.

A nation like India's biggest issue is unemployment. Young people should be prepared for relevant employment through vocational education, especially for skilled and semi-skilled traders. Any educational intervention should aim to ensure that the targeted beneficiaries participate in the programme and gain the necessary reading and numeracy skills as well as higher-order cognitive talents such as values and moral judgement as well as emotional intelligence. According to our former president Dr. A P J Abdul Kalam (2002), an integrated developmental plant and empowered management structures in the sphere of education are among the most crucial requirements of the country while it is in a development mode. He continued by saying that by bringing human thought into alignment with the balance of the cosmos, our educational system should work to produce enlightened people who are a combination of learning and values. (Dhanya Krishna, 2012).

Kothari Commission (1964-1966) emphasized fields, so that students can take up certain vocation without going for purposeless education. The inclusion of work experience as a mandatory component of all educational programmes is also advised. Work experience is described as "participation in productive work in school, at home, in the workshop, on a farm, in a factory, or in any other productive environment." Education is meant to enlighten people with the knowledge and skills to improve their lives as well as the values and attitudes to live together. It is one of the most important components in the growth of a nation. The panel stated: "There is a need to provide some corrective to the overly academic aspect of formal education." It made a clear distinction between work experience in education and vocational lysing education. It might facilitate young people's transition into the world of employment. It could contribute to the increase in national productivity both by helping students develop insights into productive processes and generating in them the habit of hard and responsible work there by strengthening the links between the individual and community the educated persons and the masses. (Roy, 2009)

Working and learning can always be connected, according to the Ishwar Bhai Patel Committee report from1977, which stated that the curriculum should be able to connect learning closely to socially beneficial physical labour and the socioeconomic position of the nation.

The aim of curricular area is to provide children with opportunities of participating in social and economic activities inside and outside the classroom. It must not be confined to the four walls of the school nor can they be provided by the teacher only. Program should, therefore be so planned and implemented that the local community, community development, organisations and government agencies participate in the and co-operate with the school. (Jayaprakash, 2015)

The national review committee on upper secondary education completely embraced the SUPW concept proposed by the Iswarbhai Patel committee, with a particular emphasis on the vocationalization of education for the +2 level (Adiseshiah Committee, Govt. of India, 1978). Since the national education strategy of 1986 was more focused on students' entry into the workforce than anything else, vocational training in higher secondary schools received a lot of attention. However, rather than acting as a powerful catalyst for the activation of information that is useful to society and the development of creative and motivated citizens, the goal of work experience is more to build the workforce, strength, and vocational education.

The NCF-2005 identified knowledge work-centred pedagogy as a crucial method of reconstructing the current school education system in its Focus Group paper on work and education at knowledge workplaces. According to this policy, work will be woven throughout the curriculum with the aim of integrating productive work alongside all other types of work (such as activities, experiments, surveys, field-based study, and social action) in the core curriculum as a means of acquiring knowledge and fostering the development of skills, values, and other generic competencies. (Roy, 2009)

Thus, it is evident from above that productive work has always been at knowledge in various policy and curriculum documents as possibly the most significant aspect of pedagogic medium in India.

Obstacles could be economic, technological, societal, or personal, and they face the entire world. To handle the challenges, the educational system needs to be flexible and adaptable. Based on broader concepts of young people's capacities and enhanced communication skills, researchers emphasise the need for a stronger emphasis on stimulating creativity in learning. New methods must be developed in order to increase students' motivation, self-esteem, and skill levels. We would rather emphasise uniqueness more than any of these things since it can only develop when learning freedom is promoted. This means that we should place a strong emphasis on the entire development of each person's potential, including their capacity for original thought and reasoning, creativity, innovation, and entrepreneurship. The council's recommendations on how to best enhance education's role in a fully functional knowledge triangle encourage educational and training institutions to make sure that all levels of instruction and testing promote entrepreneurship, innovation, and creativity. (Jayaprakash, 2015)

The importance of including entrepreneurship education in the educational environment, particularly in the School Education curriculum, has been emphasised by A.P.J. Abdul Kalam. According to him, the main goal of education in a nation like index is to maximise the potential of our people resource and gradually convert it into a knowledge society. The education system should start putting challenges in place as soon as possible and should be fully prepared to take part in societal development. When students leave educational institutions, the education system should actively develop their entrepreneurial skills and occupational aptitudes in them. They should have the confidence to launch their own small businesses and be given the training to do so.

The corporate world is dynamic and the changes or to serve that is a series of new concept and techniques are fast coming into being and the earlier and traditional ones are becoming obsolete. This situation has given rise to the need for restructuring the curriculum of Commerce Education of all level so as to make it meaningful and compatible with the concept and techniques among the commerce teachers of further channelize and streamline their contribution

THEORETICAL OVERVIEW OF THE STUDY

Our lifestyle has been revolutionised by commerce, which has also profoundly changed our attitudes, outlooks, and other aspects of our thinking. We can see the effects of trade all around us. In such a crucial area as health, communication, transportation, and power, among others, commerce has brought about change. Since the average lifespan of people has doubled, it can be claimed without any hesitation that we owe our very existence to business. Commerce is a global phenomenon with enormous material advantages and educational impacts. The industrialization of agriculture and the discharge of nuclear energy are significant. Commerce has made a significant contribution to culture in addition to its commitment to financial gain. Actually, speaking, the modern world is being preserved through commerce. (Dhanya, 2012)

It is essential to give students knowledge of various functional areas of business and related activities so they can be shaped in accordance with the changing demands of trade, commerce, and industry. Commerce education is a branch of knowledge that gives its learners experience with the business world broadly and in all of its manifestations. The fundamental goal of commerce education is to deliver high quality learning in accordance with the demands of the student, including their abilities, aptitude, and interests for integrating their learning with real-life situations. One can acquire a solid foundation of knowledge in specialised fields like accountancy, management, business studies, economics, insurance, banking and finance, marketing, entrepreneurship, etc. with a commerce education. Additionally, it imparts practical skills for navigating the world of commerce, including how to choose the best means of transportation, gather financial data, and conduct audits. According to Chesseman (1904) "commerce education is that form of instruction with both directly and indirectly prepared the Businessman for his calling".

With the emergence of new industries like financial services, consulting, and business process outsourcing, the entire economy is undergoing a significant transition, and the service sector is outpacing the industrial sector. It becomes clear in this setting how important a commerce education is. In addition to teaching students' business knowledge and skills, schools must also teach them about the history of commerce and how it affects community life. It is preferable to combine liberal and vocational education in this way in order to instil practical skills while carrying out the curriculum. Education should combine the most recent technical information and connect theoretical and practical understanding to make subjects more engaging and beneficial for pupils. The emphasis should be on delineating the reasoning so that the pupils can be encouraged to solve the issues on their own. The idea is that students should learn practical skills and build entrepreneurial attitudes and values as part of their commerce education so that they would be inspired to be creative and ambitious and will start their own business rather than looking for employment. Education fosters an understanding of the economy, in which activities are interrelated to business and industry, which equips planners to pursue a career in business. Education gives a fundamental understanding of the different concepts, method, and related business practises. The goal of this integrative approach to liberal and vocational education is to encourage learners to pursue their areas of expertise. Thus, commerce should be considered both as a knowledge subject and skill subject. Commerce is that meadow of education which blows up the required knowledge, skills and attitudes for the exhilarated usage of trade, commerce and industry. Objective of commerce education is to provide both knowledge as well as skills about business related activities to the students. (Rinu, 2014)

Today's world has made commerce a part of everyone's daily lives. Everybody must now be taught about basic commerce as part of general education. Nobody objects to it being taught as a subject in schools. The same reasons that any other topic is taught in school apply to commerce as well, but it also imparts certain values that are unique to it and that no other subject can. Liberal education includes business education. Commerce learning, however, offers training in commercial outlook and aids in the development of a commercial attitude of mind in the learner, in addition to satisfying the usual needs for its inclusion as a subject in the curriculum - such as intellectual, cultural, moral, aesthetic, utilitarian, as well as vocational values. The traits that a learner acquires while studying commerce are valuable for a citizen of the world. Today, every educational system mandates the study of commerce beginning in the early grades. In the past, commerce had to fight long and hard to be given the respect it deserves in the curriculum. The worthy student was expected to study science, engineering, classics, and mathematics during a time when commerce was regarded as a subpar subject to study. New concepts or innovations in the business world were not instantly welcomed by the society and were viewed with scepticism.

Objectives of Commerce Education

- To develop skills such as conceptual skills, technical skills and application skill in the field of Commerce management and industry
- To prepare a student for a career in business as to start an enterprise of his own
- To give each student enough opportunities to acquire relevant knowledge about business and economy
- To familiarise students with the behaviour of market products as well as Finance
- To train students in the use of information technology for business
- To develop a capability in each student to identify business opportunities analyse their like return possibilities and support business development in socially desirable avenues with strong moral commitment.

Aims of Teaching Commerce

- Ability to product future economy
- Ability to compare One industrial sector with other and identify their strength and weakness.
- Analyse the financial strength of an undertaking.
- Cultivate valuable intellectual attitudes in the students.
- Teaching and acquiring ethical moral and spiritual values.
- Cultivating a forward Outlook
- Enhancing power of imagination
- Cultivating power of reasoning
- Developmental of citizenship training
- Living training to handle controversial issues.
- Ability to take to and prompt decision.
- Forecasting future conditions
- Awareness about market Trend and fluctuations
- Teaching and acquiring problem solving.

The Evolution of Entrepreneurship

The term 'entrepreneur' does not appear in the prehistory of economics. The word rooted from French during eighteenth century, and it is justified by *Savary's Dictionnaire Universel de Commerce (1723)*, which defines entrepreneur as one who undertakes a project; a manufacturer; a master builder. During fourteenth century, the word entrepreneur was called as *entreprendeur* and the term has a meaning of government contractor, usually of military fortifications or public works throughout sixteenth and seventeenth century. (Robert, 2009)

During Middle Ages, entrepreneur was given a place, usually a cleric and the functions of inventor, planner, architect, builder, manager, employer, and supervisor were the duty of him but the term does not include risk bearing and capital formation. Risk bearing is associated with entrepreneur during seventeenth century and they are responsible for the gains and losses of the business. During the 18th century entrepreneur is termed as an inventor but still they do not provide the capital. They are considered as persons who can develop new things but unable to finance their inventions by themselves. In the 19th and 20th century entrepreneurs was considered as the one who organizes, manages, and assumes the risk of a business or an enterprise. During this period, entrepreneur is the one who arrange the materials, capital and use the land for the growth of enterprise. (Robert, 2009)

In the middle of 20th century, the function of entrepreneurs is to introduce inventions and thereby recreate the pattern of production. Entrepreneurs are known as the hero for free enterprise market during 21st century. At present the role of entrepreneur is regarded as an organizer who manages, controls, systematize, purchase raw materials, arranges infrastructure and utilize resources properly in an organization.

The future of entrepreneurship will be growth with development of technologies. The modern technologies and internet have improved the ways of conduct business. Entrepreneurs now have the luxury of putting their business idea into action through the click of button.

History of Entrepreneurship

The history of entrepreneurship is a rich and multifaceted journey that spans centuries and cultures. Entrepreneurship can be traced back to ancient civilizations, and it has evolved over time in response to changing economic, technological, and social landscapes. Here's an overview of the history of entrepreneurship:

- **Ancient Civilization:** Entrepreneurship can be evident in the earliest human cultures, as members of these communities engaged in trade, craftsmanship, and agricultural pursuits. Mesopotamian tradesmen, Silk Road merchants, and maritime Phoenicians are among examples.
- **Middle Ages:** Europe experienced the emergence of guilds and trade groups during this time, which gave artisans and craftsmen a framework for cooperation and the defence of their interests. Modern business procedures were built on the foundation of these early types of organised entrepreneurship.
- **Industrial Revolution (18th-19th centuries):** The Industrial Revolution brought about significant technological advancements,

leading to the rise of factories and mass production. Entrepreneurs like Richard Arkwright and James Watt played pivotal roles in developing new technologies and transforming industries.

- **19th Century:** The 19th century saw the expansion of entrepreneurship with the advent of railroads, telegraphs, and global trade. Entrepreneurs like Andrew Carnegie, John D. Rockefeller, and Cornelius Vanderbilt amassed vast fortunes by capitalizing on these advancements.
- **20th Century:** The 20th century marked a period of rapid industrialization, innovation, and globalization. Entrepreneurs like Henry Ford revolutionized manufacturing with the assembly line, while individuals like Steve Jobs and Bill Gates transformed the technology landscape with personal computers and software.
- **Post-World War II:** The aftermath of World War II saw the emergence of new industries and the growth of small and medium-sized enterprises (SMEs). Government policies, such as funding programs and incentives, contributed to the expansion of entrepreneurship across various sectors.
- **Digital Age:** The late 20th and early 21st centuries brought about the digital revolution, with the internet and advancements in communication technology changing the way businesses operate. The rise of e-commerce, social media, and tech startups created new opportunities for entrepreneurs.
- **Social Entrepreneurship:** In recent decades, a growing emphasis on social and environmental issues has led to the rise of social entrepreneurship. These entrepreneurs focus on creating businesses that address societal challenges while generating profits.
- **Globalization:** The interconnectedness of economies and cultures through globalization has enabled entrepreneurs to access markets and resources worldwide. This has led to the growth of multinational corporations and a diverse range of entrepreneurial ventures.
- **Innovation and Disruption:** The 21st century has seen an increasing focus on innovation and disruption. Entrepreneurs are leveraging emerging technologies like artificial intelligence, block chain, and biotechnology to create novel solutions and transform industries.

Throughout history, entrepreneurship has played a pivotal role in driving economic growth, technological progress, and societal change. It continues to evolve in response to the dynamic nature of the global economy and the ever-changing needs and desires of consumers.

The concept of Entrepreneurship & Entrepreneurship Education.

History of Entrepreneurship Education

Entrepreneurship education has evolved significantly over the years in response to changing economic, social, and technological landscapes. Here's a brief overview of its history:

- **Early Roots (Late 19th to Early 20th Century):** The concept of entrepreneurship education can be traced back to the late 19th and early 20th centuries. Land-grant universities in the United States, such as Cornell University and the University of Wisconsin, offered agricultural and engineering courses that indirectly fostered entrepreneurial skills by providing practical knowledge to students.
- **Mid-20th Century:** In the mid-20th century, entrepreneurship education was often informal and centred around mentorship and apprenticeships. However, it wasn't widely recognized as a formal field of study.
- **Late 20th Century:** The late 20th century saw the emergence of business schools and university programs that began to offer more structured entrepreneurship education. The University of California, Los Angeles (UCLA) established one of the first formal entrepreneurship programs in 1971. The focus during this period was often on small business management.
- **1980s and 1990s:** With the rise of technology and the start-up culture, the need for specialized entrepreneurship education became more apparent. Business schools around the world began to offer courses and programs specifically geared toward teaching students how to start and manage innovative ventures. The Babson College in Massachusetts became a pioneer in entrepreneurship education during this era.
- **21st Century:** Entrepreneurship education continued to evolve in the 21st century to reflect the changing dynamics of the global economy. The focus shifted from merely teaching business management to fostering creativity, innovation, and problem-solving skills. This period also saw the rise of dedicated entrepreneurship centres, incubators, and accelerators within universities and in the private sector. Online education platforms further democratized access to entrepreneurship education.
- **Integrated Approach:** Entrepreneurship education gradually started being integrated into various academic disciplines beyond business schools. Engineering, design, and liberal arts programs began to incorporate entrepreneurship principles to encourage interdisciplinary thinking and innovation.

- **Experiential Learning:** Hands-on learning, such as internships, startup competitions, and real-world projects, became a central aspect of modern entrepreneurship education. Students were encouraged to apply theoretical knowledge in practical settings.
- **Globalization:** As economies became more interconnected, entrepreneurship education began to emphasize global perspectives. Cross-cultural understanding, international market dynamics, and the ability to operate in diverse environments became crucial skills for aspiring entrepreneurs.
- **Social Entrepreneurship:** The 21st century also saw the rise of social entrepreneurship, focusing on ventures that address societal challenges. Many educational institutions started incorporating social impact elements into their entrepreneurship curricula.
- **Tech Entrepreneurship and Innovation:** With the rapid advancement of technology, tech entrepreneurship and innovation became prominent themes in entrepreneurship education. Universities and programs dedicated to fostering technology startups gained traction.
- **Online Resources:** The proliferation of online courses, webinars, and educational platforms provided even broader access to entrepreneurship education. Renowned universities and successful entrepreneurs began sharing their knowledge through digital channels.

Overall, the history of entrepreneurship education reflects the changing nature of business, technology, and society. It has evolved from informal mentorships to structured academic programs that encompass various disciplines and emphasize practical application, creativity, and global perspectives.

When compared to other sub-disciplines of education, entrepreneurship education is a new and young field. It is considered that the concept of entrepreneurship education is emerged in 20th century because there is difficulty in determining the beginning of entrepreneurship education as an academic field and as teaching practice. In today's never changing workplace, entrepreneurship education is a vehicle for teaching students to look for a need or a problem and create a solution. Entrepreneurship education is made up of all kinds of experiences that give student a vision on how to access different types of opportunities. It is expected from the teacher to encourage students to look for entrepreneurial opportunities for themselves. This is the objective of entrepreneurship education in the general school education curriculum. (Gustav, 2021)

"Entrepreneurship should not be a mystery to our youth, but an integral part of the normal curriculum exposure to the learning process. Youth

Entrepreneurship and small business are the future of our province and country" views Bob Boxter, ManagingDirector, true end district channels of Commerce, NovaScotia, Canada.

The term "entrepreneur" in the modern sense came into usage in the late 18th century with the advent of the Industrial Revolution in England. It was during this period that people demonstrated an innovative spirit. They developed inventions and made an appreciable number of discoveries in a variety of productive occupations. Their innovative behaviour engaged them in doing new and useful things or old things in an improved way. The invention of colour photography and colour television, for example, were the responses of innovative efforts of individuals who conceived the idea, developed it and pursued it to its ultimate success. These innovators came to be known as entrepreneurs. (Gustav, 2021)

The concept of entrepreneurship is a complex phenomenon. Broadly it relates to the entrepreneur, his or her vision and the implementation. The key player is the entrepreneur. Entrepreneurship refers to a process of action an entrepreneur undertakes to establish in his or her Enterprise. It is a creative and innovative response to the environment which is the societal of actions to further the interest of the entrepreneur.

John Kunkel considered entrepreneurship as a function of social, political, and economic structure. Max Weber treated it as a function of religious beliefs. The concept of entrepreneurship involves four elements. (Abraham, 2010) They are:

- **Organising:** Organising involves mobilization of resources and utilization of them to initiate, maintain, or enhance profit by the production or supply of goods and services. Entrepreneurs also mobilize other factors of production such as land, labour and capital
- **Risk – bearing:** Starting a new enterprise always involves risk. The enterprise may earnprofit or incur loss. The entrepreneurs should be bold enough to assume this risk.
- **Vision:** Entrepreneurial vision encompasses the relentless pursuit of operational excellence, innovative technology, and responsiveness to the needs of the market.
- **Innovation:** Innovation refers to introduction of something new in the economy. The innovation may be related to new products, modern technology, new sources of raw material, new market or new organisation.

Entrepreneurship is a composite skill, the resultant of a mix of many qualities and traits. These include imagination, readiness to take risks, ability to bring together and put to use other factors of production, capital, labour, land as also intangible factors such as the ability to mobilize scientific and technological advances. Thus, entrepreneurship is the propensity of mind to take calculated risk with confidence to achieve predetermined business or industrial objective. In substance, it is the risk-taking ability of the individual, broadly coupled with the correct decision making.

Government must play two different types of functions in every economic system: promotional and regulatory responsibilities. Government must possess a particular level of expertise and understanding to support various economic activity in both roles. Few people who are directly involved in government activities are able to promote all of them. To ensure the development of the economy from all angles, the economy as a whole should engage in all government actions. Now an entrepreneur becomes important. Every member of society with entrepreneurial abilities will be able to participate in society and make a contribution to the expansion of the economy. The government in this situation must take an active role in fostering the development of the people's entrepreneurial talents. Since the development of the economy depends on the development of entrepreneurial talents, it is more important than ever to use every person's potential to advance economic activity. Since small businesses account for a greater proportion of global business operations, it follows that all economies make full use of entrepreneurial abilities. Today's managed economies are also becoming more open to the market economy so that those economies' people resources can use their entrepreneurial abilities. The entrepreneurial skills of the residents of such an economy must therefore be used for economic progress, whether it is a controlled economy or an open economy, and they should be permitted to play independently. Government should play the promotional role to assist the small business people to contribute their mite to develop the economy. This is the relevance of an entrepreneur in an economy. (Anjali, 2019)

Economic development of any region is an outcome of purposeful human activity. Men assume various roles in the development process, namely, organiser of human capital, natural material resources, worker and consumer. He stands at the centre of the whole process of economic development. According to Schumpeter, economic development consists of "employing resources in a different way" in doing a new combination of means of production. The entrepreneur locates ideas and put them into effect in the process of economic development.

Since entrepreneurship is linked to innovation and the development of something new, it is frequently equated with starting a new firm and, as a result, with business ownership. However, entrepreneurship can also exist outside of the economic world or in very huge organisations. In fact, the importance of entrepreneurial behaviour in our society has increased. where employees must deal with a more unpredictable work environment, multiple job changes throughout their careers, increased chances of being self-employed, and duties that increasingly call for traits like independence, initiative, and creativity.People with these entrepreneurial traits are better equipped to adapt to and participate in rapid social and economic change. Consequently, both entrepreneurship and the educational system are crucial for economic growth from a society standpoint. However, the value of education for business has only lately come to light. Education has been cited as one of the factors affecting a nation's degree of entrepreneurial activity while developing a framework for explaining entrepreneurship. The educational system has historically prevented the growth of entrepreneurial traits because it teaches children to obey, repeat information, and work for wages after they graduate from school. Entrepreneurs, on the other hand, frequently rely on their own judgement, learn via trial and error, and develop and facilitate their own opportunities. (Jayaprakash, 2015)

Entrepreneurship is associated with diversity among individuals who have a range of interests, points of view, and personality characteristics as well as with opening up opportunities in unpredictably changing environments. Because modern societies rely on variety to function, these distinctions are appreciated. Scholars and policymakers alike are finally acknowledging the importance of the educational system for entrepreneurship. The educational system assists people in being more aware of their alternatives by enlarging their horizons and educating them about different work options. Additionally, it equips them with the resources they need to cooperate as well as see and capture business opportunities.

Why is entrepreneurship education in schools a hot topic right now? The short answer is that because society today demands more and more entrepreneurial behaviour, it is more probable that the younger generation will work in organisations that are more entrepreneurially oriented in the future. This will only increase the country's entrepreneurial activity. The planning commission's projections, which aim to create 10 crore jobs over the next ten years, highly endorsed self-employment as a solution for the plethora of unemployed youth. The high rate of entrepreneurship in India is attributed to the country's high unemployment rate, and it may not be sustained without the aid of the appropriate educational framework. The research emphasised the necessity to forge a strong connection between the spirit of entrepreneurship and education after observing that India's education system is incapable of fostering entrepreneurial orientation among people. (Roy, 2009)

Entrepreneurial Competencies

According to a recent study, it was found out that position of certain competencies for abilities result in superior performance. An entrepreneur may possess certain competencies and at the same time it is possible to develop these through training, experience and guidance. various competencies required for superior performance were identified during the study and are as under.

- **Initiative:** It is an inner urge in an individual to do or initiate something. there is popular saying "well begun is half done." It is the Entrepreneur who takes aur initiates the first move towards setting up of an enterprise. Most of the innovators have got this urge to do something different. Entrepreneur basically is an innovator who carries out new combinations to initiate and accelerate the process of economic development
- **Looking for opportunity:** An entrepreneur is always on the lookout or searching for opportunity and is ready to exploit it in the best interest of the organisation.
- **Persistence:** An entrepreneur is never disheartened by failures. He believes in the Japanese proverb 'Fall seven times stand up eight'. He follows try- try again for overcoming the obstacles that come in the way of achieving goals.
- **Information seeker:** A successful entrepreneur always keeps his eyes and ear open and is receptive to new ideas which can help him in realising his goals. He is ready to consult expert for getting their expert advice.
- **Quality consciousness:** Successful entrepreneur does not believe in moderate or average performance. They said high quality standards for themselves and then put in their best for achieving these standards. They believe in excellence, which is reflected in everything they do.
- **Commitment to work:** Successful entrepreneurs are preferred to make all sacrifices for honouring the commitments they have made. Whatever they commit, take it as a moral binding for honouring their commitments, irrespective of the cost involved.
- **Commitment to efficiency:** Top performers are always keen to revise new methods aimed at promoting efficiency. They are keen to evolve and try new methods in that making working easier, simpler, better and economical.
- **Proper planning:** successful entrepreneur developed for your future cause of action keeping in mind the goals to be realised. They believe in developing relevant and realistic plants and denture proper execution of the same in their pursuit of attaining their goals.
- **Problem solver:** Successful entrepreneur take problem was a challenge and put in their best for finding out the most appropriate

solution for the same. They will faster for understand the problem and then evolve appropriate strategy for overcoming the problem.

- **Self-confidence:** Top performers are not cowed down by difficulties as they believe in their own abilities and strengths. they have full faith on their knowledge, skill and competencies and are not worried about future uncertainties.
- **Assertive:**An assertive person knows what to say, when to say, how to say and whom to say. He believes in his abilities and ensures that others fall in line with his thinking, aimed at promoting the interest of the organisation.
- **Persuasive:** A successful entrepreneur through his sound arguments on the logical reasoning is in a position to convince others to do the works the way he wants them to do. It is not physical but intellectual force he will use for convincing others.
- **Effective monitoring:** Top performers ensure that everything is carried out in their organisations ask for their wishes. They ensure regular monitoring of the working so that the goals of the organisation are achieved in best possible manner.
- **Employees welfare:** Future of the organisation depends on its employees. If the employees are dedicated, committed a loyal, the organisation is bound to perform well. A successful entrepreneur tries to promote organisations in rest through promotion of interest of the workers. He takes personal interest in solving problems confronting workers and generates the feeling that there is interdependence of the interest of workers and the management.
- **Affective strategies:** A successful entrepreneur process is the ability to evolve relevant strategy, aimed at safeguarding or promoting organisations interest.

Characteristics of Entrepreneurs

An individual can start a new business or a venture with the help of proper utilization of his/her talents. He purchased the required raw materials, produce the finished products, processing or distributing the finished goods and services to the society. The qualities like adventurism, innovation, risk taking, creativity is enriched within an entrepreneur. The entrepreneur will be the one who always puts up new projects, creates employment opportunities, and thereby paves the way for the growth of other sectors. In short, the entrepreneur is a person who brings in overall changes through innovation with a view to attaining social good. An entrepreneur who has a high level of administrative capability, fair and ability for decision making, computationalskill, delegationskill, organisationalskills, good at communication and has a sound technical knowledge stands a much better chance of success than his counterpart who possesses none or a low level of these basic qualities. It is the possession of these scarce qualities which confers advantage on some people in becoming an entrepreneur. Besides these qualities, however, the entrepreneur also needs either to be himself a generalist so that he can discharge his function without delegation, aur to possess delegation and organisational skills. The Characteristics of an entrepreneur that contribute to success are the result of his achievement motivation.

- **Mental ability:** Mental ability consists of intelligence and creative thinking. An entrepreneur must be reasonably intelligent, and should have creative thinking and must be able to engage in the analysis of various problems and situations in order to deal with them. The entrepreneur should anticipate changes and must be able to study the various situations under which decisions have to be made.
- **Clear objective:** An entrepreneur should have a clear objective as to the exact nature of the business, the nature of the goods to be produced and subsidiary activities to be undertaken. A successful entrepreneur may have the objective to establish the product, to make profit or to render social service.
- **Business secrecy:** An entrepreneur must be able to guard business secrets. Leakage of business secrets to trade competitions is a serious matter which should be carefully guarded against by an entrepreneur. An entrepreneur should be able to make a proper selection of his assistants.
- **Human relation ability:** The most important personality factors contributing to the success of an entrepreneur are emotional stability, personalrelations, consideration and tactfulness. An entrepreneur must maintain good relation with his customers is he is to establish the relations that will encourage them to continue to patronise his business. He must also maintain good relations with his employees if he is to motivate them to perform their jobs at a high level of efficiency. An entrepreneur who maintains good relations with the customer, employees, suppliers, creditors and the community are much more likely to succeed in his business than the individual who does not invest in maintaining these relations.
- **Communication ability:** This ability pertains to communicate effectively. Good communication also means that both the sender and the receiver understand each other and are being understood. An entrepreneur who can effectively communicate

with customers, employees, suppliers and creditors will be more likely to succeed that the entrepreneur who does not.

- **Technical knowledge:** An entrepreneur must have a responsible level of technical knowledge. This is the vulnerability that most people are able to acquire if they try hard enough.

Robert D. Hirsch Has identified a few more capability as your personal characteristics that an entrepreneur should possess. According to him, the entrepreneur must have an adequate commitment, motivation and skills to start and build a business. the entrepreneur must determine if the management team have the necessary complementary skills to succeed. some key characteristics of a successful entrepreneur are.

- **Motivator:** An entrepreneur must build a team, keep it motivated and provide an environment for individual growth and career development.
- **Self-confidence:** Entrepreneurs must have believed in themselves and their ability to achieve their goals.
- **Long term involvement:** An entrepreneur must be committed to the project with the time Horizon of five to seven years. No ninety-day wonders are allowed.
- **High energy level:** Success of an entrepreneur demands the ability to work long hours for sustained periods of time.
- **Persistent problem solver:** An entrepreneur must have an intense desire to complete a task or solve a problem. Creativity is an essential ingredient.
- **Initiative:** Entrepreneur must have initiative, accepting personal responsibility for action and above or make good use of resources.
- **Goal setter:** An entrepreneur must be able to set challenging but realistic goals.
- **Moderate risk taker:** An entrepreneur must be a moderate risk taker and learn from failures.

Functions of an Entrepreneur

The main entrepreneurial functions can be summarised in to the following:

- **Innovation:** Innovation simply refers to the process of finding out new things. Inentrepreneurship innovation may take the following forms: Introduction of new product, Introduction of a new method of production, finding new markets for the products, finding new and cheaper sources of supply of raw materials, Making alterations in the organization management.

- **Risk -bearing:** Risk is the common factor of every business. 'No risk, no profit' is the common Fact that is associated with every business. Bearing of risk refers to the willingness of a person to face the losses arising from the uncertainties that emerged in the business bravely. The success of an entrepreneur depends mainly on predicting the uncertainties and thereby minimising the losses. Whenever an entrepreneur is making an innovation, he/she must be vigilant of the unexpected risks inherent in it.
- **Organising and managing the enterprise:** Organising involves bringing together various factors of production such as men, material, and money. As an entrepreneur proper organising helps to reduce the cost of production and thus the objective of the organisation can be achieved (maximisation of profit). The entrepreneurs are responsible to take the decisions at the initial stages of organising an enterprise and in later stages he/she can delegate their authority to subordinates. But the fact is that an entrepreneur can only transfer his/her authority to the subordinates, the responsibility is always lies within them. There must be a close supervision from the part of an entrepreneur on the activities performed by the subordinates. Thus, the final word regarding organisation and management should be that of the entrepreneurs.

Other Functions

Besides the above, the entrepreneur performs the following functions also:

- **Exploring market opportunities:** Entrepreneurs always need to seek advice of experts in the concerned field in order to market the products in the competitive market because the function of marketing is always creating problems to a new entrepreneur.
- **Mobilization of production resources:** Mobilization of production resources minimises difficulties in production and reduces cost of production and helps the entrepreneur earn more. The resources mobilized by the entrepreneur must be sufficient to produce quality goods which can compete with other products in the market.
- **Managing Finance:** There should be a proper financial planning from the part of an entrepreneur because they are the one who takes important financial decisions such as total capital investment, sources of funds to be invested, borrowing of fund when there is a shortage and also find the agencies engaged in industrial finance.
- **Managing production process:** Efficient management in the production process helps the entrepreneur in the reduction of cost of production, improvement of quality of products, better quality

of products, better utilization of factors of production, minimisation of wastages and profitable employment of labour force.

- **Dealing with Government matters:** The entrepreneur has to deal with many governmental matters like industrial licensing, sales tax and income tax. Proper advice from experts in the concerned field can be sought by the entrepreneur.
- **Maintaining Management –Employee relations:** The entrepreneur has to maintain a proper management – employee relations because the strength of an organisation is always depending on its human resources. They should be treated as human beings, the absence of which will cause employee unrest and dissatisfaction.

Entrepreneurial Traits

An entrepreneur needs intuition, creative thinking and innovative ability. Entrepreneurs were not born; they learned to become entrepreneurs. They can learn and improve their traits through various training programmes for entrepreneurs. The following traits are required for an entrepreneur.

Conceptual Traits

An entrepreneur has the ability to identify relationships quickly in the midst of complex situations. He identifies problems and begins to work in their solution faster than other people. The conceptual traits of an entrepreneur encompass a combination of characteristics, skills, and attitudes that contribute to the ability to identify, create, and capitalize on business opportunities. While there is no one-size-fits-all definition of an entrepreneur, several key conceptual traits are commonly associated with successful entrepreneurial endeavours:

- **Vision and Innovation:** Entrepreneurs often possess a forward-thinking vision and a willingness to challenge the status quo. They are adept at identifying opportunities for innovation and are driven to create new products, services, or solutions.
- **Risk-taking:** Entrepreneurship inherently involves risk, and successful entrepreneurs are comfortable taking calculated risks. They understand that failure is a possibility but see it as a learning experience rather than a setback.
- **Resilience:** The ability to bounce back from setbacks and failures is crucial for entrepreneurs. Resilience helps them navigate challenges, adapt to changes, and persevere in the face of adversity.
- **Adaptability:** Entrepreneurs operate in dynamic environments, and the ability to adapt to changing circumstances is vital. Flexibility and a willingness to adjust strategies based on feedback and market conditions contribute to long-term success.

- **Passion and Drive:** Entrepreneurs are often fuelled by a passion for their ideas or a particular industry. This passion sustains their motivation and drives them to overcome obstacles, work long hours, and stay committed to their goals.
- **Decision-making Skills:** Entrepreneurs must make numerous decisions, often with limited information and under tight deadlines. Effective decision-making involves weighing pros and cons, considering risks, and taking decisive action.
- **Resourcefulness:** Successful entrepreneurs are resourceful and can make the most of the resources available to them. This includes leveraging networks, seeking creative solutions, and optimizing efficiency.
- **Leadership and Team Building:** Entrepreneurs need strong leadership skills to inspire and guide their teams. Building a cohesive and motivated team is essential for achieving business objectives.
- **Customer Focus:** Understanding customer needs and preferences is critical for entrepreneurial success. Entrepreneurs strive to create value for their customers and build products or services that meet or exceed expectations.
- **Continuous Learning:** The business landscape is constantly evolving, and entrepreneurs must be avid learners. Staying informed about industry trends, technological advancements, and market dynamics is essential for making informed decisions.

Technical Traits

A good entrepreneur should have interest to explore new ideas, new technology and new production method. He must have a reasonable level of technical knowledge. While technical skills can vary depending on the industry and the nature of the business, here are some technical traits commonly associated with successful entrepreneurs:

- **Industry Knowledge:** Entrepreneurs need a deep understanding of the industry they operate in. This includes knowledge of market trends, competition, and the specific challenges and opportunities within their sector.
- **Technical Expertise:** Depending on the nature of their business, entrepreneurs may need technical expertise in areas such as software development, engineering, manufacturing processes, or other specialized fields.
- **Financial Literacy:** Entrepreneurs should have a good understanding of financial principles, including budgeting, financial

forecasting, and managing cash flow. This knowledge is essential for making informed business decisions.

- **Digital Literacy:** In today's digital age, entrepreneurs need to be proficient in using technology. This includes understanding digital marketing, e-commerce platforms, social media, and other online tools relevant to their business.
- **Data Analysis:** Analysing data is essential for making informed decisions. Entrepreneurs should be comfortable interpreting data, using analytics tools, and leveraging insights to improve business strategies.
- **Project Management:** Entrepreneurs often juggle multiple projects simultaneously. Effective project management skills, including planning, organization, and resource allocation, are crucial for ensuring tasks are completed on time and within budget.
- **Risk Management:** Entrepreneurs must be able to assess and manage risks associated with their business. This includes understanding potential pitfalls, implementing risk mitigation strategies, and being adaptable in the face of uncertainty.
- **Technical Innovation:** Entrepreneurs who lead in innovation need to stay abreast of technological advancements relevant to their industry. Being open to new ideas and technologies can give them a competitive edge.
- **Networking Skills:** While not purely technical, the ability to build and leverage a network is critical for entrepreneurs. This network can provide technical expertise, mentorship, and potential business partnerships.

Human Relation

An entrepreneur should maintain good relations with his customers and public. He must also maintain good relations with his employees to motivate them to higher levels of efficiency.Here are some common human relations traits often associated with successful entrepreneurs:

- **Communication Skills:** Entrepreneurs need to effectively communicate their ideas, vision, and goals to various stakeholders, including employees, customers, investors, and partners.
- **Empathy:** Understanding and relating to the needs and feelings of others is crucial for building strong relationships. Empathetic entrepreneurs can better connect with employees, customers, and collaborators.
- **Team Building:** Successful entrepreneurs know how to build and lead effective teams. They understand the strengths and

weaknesses of team members and create an environment that fosters collaboration and productivity.

- **Networking Skills:** Entrepreneurs often need to establish and maintain a network of contacts. Building and nurturing relationships with other professionals, mentors, and industry peers can provide valuable support, advice, and business opportunities.
- **Conflict Resolution:** Entrepreneurs encounter conflicts in various aspects of their business. Those who excel in human relations can navigate conflicts diplomatically, finding solutions that satisfy all parties involved.
- **Adaptability:** The ability to adapt to different personalities, work styles, and changing business environments is crucial. Entrepreneurs who can navigate diverse situations with ease are more likely to build successful and lasting relationships.
- **Leadership:** Entrepreneurs need strong leadership skills to inspire and guide their teams. Leadership involves setting a positive example, motivating others, and providing clear direction.
- **Trustworthiness:** Building trust is fundamental in business relationships. Entrepreneurs who are honest, reliable, and uphold their commitments are more likely to earn the trust of employees, customers, and partners.
- **Positive Attitude:** Maintaining a positive attitude in the face of challenges can influence the overall atmosphere within a business. Optimistic entrepreneurs are better equipped to motivate and inspire their teams.
- **Cultural Sensitivity:** In an increasingly globalized world, entrepreneurs may interact with people from diverse cultural backgrounds. Being culturally sensitive helps in building respectful and effective relationships with individuals from different parts of the world.

Communication

Communication of an entrepreneur must be to the point, crisp and convincing. Communication ability is the secret of the success of most entrepreneurs.Here are some key communication traits that successful entrepreneurs often possess:

- **Clarity:** Entrepreneurs need to convey their ideas, vision, and goals clearly to team members, investors, and other stakeholders. Clarity in communication helps in avoiding misunderstandings and ensures that everyone is on the same page.

- **Active Listening:** Entrepreneurs should be adept at listening to others, including employees, customers, and partners. Active listening allows them to understand concerns, gather valuable insights, and make informed decisions.
- **Adaptability:** Communication styles may need to be adapted to different audiences and situations. Whether addressing employees, negotiating with partners, or presenting to investors, entrepreneurs should be able to adjust their communication approach accordingly.
- **Transparency:** Successful entrepreneurs often maintain transparency in their communication. Sharing information about the company's performance, challenges, and future plans helps build trust with stakeholders and fosters a positive working environment.
- **Negotiation Skills:** Entrepreneurs frequently engage in negotiations, whether it's with suppliers, clients, or investors. Effective negotiation involves clear communication of expectations, compromise, and finding mutually beneficial solutions.
- **Inspiration and Motivation:** Entrepreneurs often need to inspire and motivate their team. They should be able to communicate a compelling vision, instil confidence, and keep team members motivated during challenging times.
- **Networking Skills:** Building and maintaining a professional network is essential for entrepreneurs. Effective networking involves clear and concise communication to establish meaningful connections, partnerships, and collaborations.
- **Feedback Mechanism:** Entrepreneurs should create an environment that encourages open communication and feedback. Constructive feedback helps in continuous improvement and fosters a culture of learning within the organization.
- **Crisis Communication:** In times of crisis, clear and timely communication is crucial. Entrepreneurs should be able to address issues transparently, provide reassurance, and outline plans for overcoming challenges.
- **Digital Communication:** In today's digital age, entrepreneurs need to be proficient in various digital communication channels, including email, social media, and collaboration tools. Clear and concise written communication is especially important.
- **Emotional Intelligence:** Entrepreneurs with high emotional intelligence can navigate interpersonal relationships effectively. Understanding and managing emotions, both their own and others', contributes to successful communication and leadership.

Decision-making

It means the ability to choose the correct alternative from a number of alternatives. An entrepreneur should have the ability to analyse the various aspects of the business to arrive at a decision.Entrepreneurs often possess a unique set of traits that influence their decision-making processes. While individuals vary, some common decision-making traits among successful entrepreneurs include:

- **Risk-taking propensity:** Entrepreneurs are typically comfortable with taking calculated risks. They understand that uncertainty is inherent in business, and they are willing to take well-thought-out risks to achieve their goals.
- **Decisiveness:** Entrepreneurs often need to make quick decisions in dynamic environments. Being decisive allows them to respond rapidly to changing circumstances and capitalize on opportunities.
- **Adaptability:** The business landscape is ever-changing, and successful entrepreneurs are adaptable. They can adjust their strategies and decisions based on new information, market shifts, or unexpected challenges.
- **Visionary thinking:** Entrepreneurs often have a clear vision of where they want to take their businesses. This vision guides their decision-making, helping them make choices that align with their long-term goals.
- **Resilience:** Entrepreneurship is filled with ups and downs. Resilient entrepreneurs bounce back from failures, learn from setbacks, and use these experiences to inform their future decisions.
- **Customer focus:** Understanding customer needs and preferences is crucial for success. Entrepreneurs who prioritize customer-centric decision-making are more likely to create products or services that meet market demands.
- **Analytical skills:** Entrepreneurs need to analyse data, market trends, and various factors to make informed decisions. Strong analytical skills enable them to assess risks and opportunities more effectively.
- **Creativity:** Entrepreneurs often face unique challenges that require creative solutions. The ability to think outside the box allows them to innovate and differentiate their businesses in competitive markets.
- **Persistence:** Building a successful business takes time and effort. Entrepreneurs who are persistent in pursuing their goals are more likely to overcome obstacles and make the necessary decisions to keep moving forward.

- **Resourcefulness:** Entrepreneurs are often resourceful, finding ways to achieve their objectives even when faced with constraints. This trait is valuable in decision-making, especially when dealing with limited resources.
- **Networking skills:** Building and maintaining a network is crucial for an entrepreneur. Networking provides access to valuable information, mentorship, and collaboration opportunities that can inform and enhance decision-making.

Time Management

Time management is the act or process of exercising continuous control over time spent on specific activities. This is necessary to increase efficiency or productivity. An entrepreneur must possess the trait to manage the time.Effective time management is a crucial trait for entrepreneurs as it directly impacts their productivity, the success of their ventures, and their overall well-being. Here are some key aspects of the time management trait in successful entrepreneurs:

- **Prioritization:** Entrepreneurs need to identify and prioritize tasks based on their importance and urgency. This involves distinguishing between tasks that contribute directly to the growth of the business and those that are less critical.
- **Goal Setting:** Successful entrepreneurs set clear and achievable short-term and long-term goals. This helps them stay focused on what needs to be accomplished and provides a sense of direction for their efforts.
- **Effective Planning:** Planning involves breaking down larger goals into smaller, manageable tasks. Entrepreneurs who excel at time management create detailed plans, allocate resources efficiently, and set realistic timelines for completing tasks.
- **Delegation:** Entrepreneurs understand the importance of delegation. They delegate tasks that others can perform, allowing them to focus on strategic aspects of the business. Delegating not only saves time but also leverages the strengths of the team.
- **Time Blocking:** Entrepreneurs often use time blocking techniques to allocate specific blocks of time to different activities. This helps in maintaining focus and prevents procrastination.
- **Adaptability:** The ability to adapt to unexpected challenges and changes in the business environment is crucial. Entrepreneurs who manage their time effectively are often better equipped to handle unforeseen circumstances without compromising their overall productivity.

- **Limiting Distractions:** Entrepreneurs minimize distractions to maintain concentration during work hours. This may involve creating a dedicated workspace, turning off unnecessary notifications, or establishing specific times for checking emails and messages.
- **Continuous Learning:** Successful entrepreneurs recognize the value of continuous learning. They invest time in acquiring new skills and staying updated on industry trends, which ultimately contributes to better decision-making and business growth.
- **Work-Life Balance:** Striking a balance between work and personal life is vital for long-term success and well-being. Entrepreneurs who manage their time effectively allocate specific hours to work and also make time for relaxation, family, and personal interests.
- **Reflection and Improvement:** Regularly reflecting on one's time management practices and seeking ways to improve efficiency is a characteristic of successful entrepreneurs. They learn from their experiences and adjust their strategies accordingly.

Stress Management

Stress management is one of the keys to a happy and successful life in modern society. It is the best way to manage anxiety and maintain overall well-being. Entrepreneur must adopt various mechanisms to control the level of stress. Stress management is a crucial trait for entrepreneurs, as they often face a myriad of challenges and uncertainties in the dynamic business environment. Here are some key stress management traits that successful entrepreneurs often exhibit:

- **Resilience:** Entrepreneurs need to bounce back from setbacks and failures. Resilience enables them to navigate through tough times without being overwhelmed by stress. Instead of dwelling on failures, resilient entrepreneurs learn from them and use the experience to fuel future success.
- **Adaptability:** The ability to adapt to change is vital for entrepreneurs. Business environments can shift rapidly, and those who can adjust their strategies and perspectives in response to new information or challenges are better equipped to handle stress.
- **Time Management:** Entrepreneurs often face tight deadlines and multiple responsibilities. Effective time management helps them prioritize tasks, allocate resources efficiently, and avoid last-minute rushes, reducing the stress associated with tight schedules.
- **Emotional Intelligence:** Understanding and managing one's own emotions, as well as being attuned to the emotions of others, is

crucial. Entrepreneurs with high emotional intelligence can navigate interpersonal relationships more effectively, resolve conflicts, and maintain a positive work environment.

- **Problem-Solving Skills:** Entrepreneurs encounter various problems and obstacles on their journey. Those who can approach challenges with a problem-solving mindset are more likely to find effective solutions, reducing the stress associated with uncertainty and difficulty.
- **Delegate Effectively:** Entrepreneurs who try to do everything themselves often experience burnout. Effective delegation allows them to focus on their strengths and high-priority tasks while entrusting others with responsibilities, thereby reducing the overall workload and stress.
- **Healthy Lifestyle:** Maintaining a healthy lifestyle through regular exercise, proper nutrition, and sufficient sleep is essential for managing stress. Physical well-being contributes to mental resilience and the ability to cope with the demands of entrepreneurship.
- **Mindfulness and Meditation:** Incorporating mindfulness practices and meditation into daily routines can help entrepreneurs stay grounded and focused. These techniques promote relaxation, reduce anxiety, and enhance overall well-being.
- **Networking and Support Systems:** Building a strong network and having a support system, whether it's friends, family, or fellow entrepreneurs, provides outlets for sharing experiences, seeking advice, and receiving emotional support during challenging times.
- **Clear Communication:** Transparent communication helps prevent misunderstandings and reduces the stress associated with miscommunication. Entrepreneurs who can articulate their vision, expectations, and concerns effectively foster a healthier work environment.

Personality and Individual Trait

Impressive personality and individual trait help to develop entrepreneurship. These qualities are inevitable for entrepreneurs since they have to work with officers, engineers, labourers, customers, investors, Government officers, etc. However, certain characteristics are commonly associated with successful entrepreneurs. Keep in mind that these traits are not exclusive to entrepreneurs, and individuals may possess them to varying degrees. Here are some key personality traits often associated with entrepreneurs:

- **Risk-taking propensity:** Entrepreneurs are often willing to take calculated risks. They understand that uncertainty is part of the business landscape and are comfortable stepping into the unknown.
- **Vision:** Successful entrepreneurs typically have a clear vision of what they want to achieve. They can see opportunities where others might see challenges and are driven by a long-term perspective.
- **Passion and enthusiasm:** Entrepreneurs are often passionate about their ideas and projects. This passion can be contagious, helping them inspire and motivate others.
- **Resilience:** Entrepreneurship involves facing numerous challenges and setbacks. Resilient individuals can bounce back from failures, learn from them, and persist in the face of adversity.
- **Adaptability:** The business landscape is constantly evolving, and entrepreneurs need to adapt to changes in technology, market trends, and consumer preferences.
- **Creativity and innovation:** Entrepreneurs are often creative thinkers who can come up with innovative solutions to problems. They are not afraid to challenge the status quo and think outside the box.
- **Self-motivation:** Entrepreneurs are usually self-driven and don't need external forces to push them forward. They set their own goals and are intrinsically motivated to achieve them.
- **Decision-making skills:** Successful entrepreneurs are decisive and can make decisions even in the face of uncertainty. They weigh the pros and cons and take calculated risks.
- **Leadership**: Entrepreneurs often need to lead teams, and effective leadership skills are crucial. This includes the ability to communicate a compelling vision, inspire others, and delegate responsibilities.
- **Networking skills:** Building and maintaining relationships is important for entrepreneurs. Networking allows them to connect with potential partners, investors, and customers.
- **Financial literacy:** Entrepreneurs need to understand the financial aspects of their business. This includes budgeting, financial forecasting, and managing cash flow.
- **Customer focus:** Successful entrepreneurs are customer-centric. They understand the needs and preferences of their target audience and work towards delivering value to customers.

Pioneering

Entrepreneurs must explore into new opportunities. They always like discover new methods of production and new markets. Thus, they are pioneers in their own field. Entrepreneurs possess a variety of traits that contribute to their success, and one of the pioneering traits often associated with successful entrepreneurs is innovation. Innovation is the ability to think creatively, identify opportunities, and develop new solutions to address existing problems or meet emerging needs.Here are some aspects of the pioneering trait of innovation in entrepreneurs:

- **Creativity:** Entrepreneurs are often creative thinkers who can generate novel ideas and think outside the box. They are not afraid to challenge conventional wisdom and explore new ways of doing things.
- **Risk-taking:** Successful entrepreneurs are willing to take calculated risks. They understand that innovation involves uncertainty and are comfortable stepping into the unknown to pursue their ideas.
- **Adaptability:** The business landscape is dynamic, and entrepreneurs must be adaptable to changing conditions. Pioneering entrepreneurs embrace change, adjust their strategies when needed, and stay agile in the face of challenges.
- **Vision:** Entrepreneurs have a vision for the future. They can see opportunities that others might overlook and have the ability to envision a different and better reality. This vision provides them with the motivation and direction to pursue their goals.
- **Persistence:** Innovation often involves overcoming obstacles and facing failures. Pioneering entrepreneurs demonstrate persistence and resilience, learning from setbacks and using them as opportunities for growth.
- **Customer-Centric Focus:** Successful entrepreneurs understand the importance of meeting customer needs. They actively seek feedback, listen to their customers, and use this information to improve and innovate their products or services.
- **Continuous Learning:** Entrepreneurs have a mindset of continuous learning. They stay informed about industry trends, emerging technologies, and new opportunities, allowing them to stay ahead of the curve and adapt their strategies accordingly.
- **Networking:** Building and leveraging networks is crucial for entrepreneurs. Networking allows them to connect with like-minded individuals, potential collaborators, mentors, and investors, creating opportunities for collaboration and growth.
- **Resourcefulness:** Entrepreneurs often start with limited resources. The ability to be resourceful and find creative solutions to challenges is a key trait. This may involve finding innovative ways to finance a venture, bootstrap operations, or leverage existing resources more effectively.

- **Passion:** Finally, a pioneering entrepreneur is often driven by a deep passion for their idea or vision. This passion fuels their commitment, perseverance, and enthusiasm, helping them navigate the ups and downs of the entrepreneurial journey.

Unification and Organization

An entrepreneur comes in contact with many unions and organizations. He/she has to arrange many things in many ways and to unite all of them for a common goal. So, he/she must have unification and organization traits.These traits contribute to their ability to create a vision, bring people together, and execute plans effectively. Unification Traits include:

- **Visionary Leadership:** Entrepreneurs typically have a clear and compelling vision of what they want to achieve. This vision serves as a unifying force, inspiring and aligning their team toward common goals.
- **Charismatic Communication:** Entrepreneurs often excel in communication, conveying their vision in a way that motivates and engages others. They have the ability to articulate their ideas with passion and conviction, fostering a sense of unity among team members.
- **Inspirational Motivation:** Successful entrepreneurs inspire their teams by instilling a sense of purpose and significance in the work being done. This motivation helps unify individuals, creating a shared commitment to the overarching goals of the venture.
- **Risk-Taking Propensity:** Unification often involves taking calculated risks. Entrepreneurs are willing to step out of their comfort zones, encouraging their team to embrace innovation and change, thereby fostering a culture of risk-taking and adaptability.

Organizational Traits include:

- **Strategic Planning:** Entrepreneurs possess the ability to develop and implement strategic plans. This involves setting clear objectives, identifying key milestones, and creating a roadmap to guide the organization toward success.
- **Time Management:** Effectively managing time is crucial for entrepreneurs who must juggle multiple responsibilities. Prioritizing tasks, setting deadlines, and staying organized contribute to efficient time management.
- **Adaptability:** The business environment is dynamic, and successful entrepreneurs are adept at adapting to changes. This includes adjusting strategies, operations, and team structures to navigate challenges and capitalize on opportunities.

- **Team Building and Delegation:** Entrepreneurs understand the importance of building a strong team. They excel in identifying and recruiting individuals with complementary skills. Additionally, they delegate responsibilities effectively, empowering team members to contribute their expertise to the overall success of the venture.
- **Financial Management:** A key organizational trait is the ability to manage finances wisely. Entrepreneurs monitor budgets, control expenses, and make strategic financial decisions to ensure the sustainability and growth of their businesses.

Computer Knowledge

If an entrepreneur is computer literate, he/she can use the computers and software to perform different aspects of the jobs. Computer is a helpful tool for decision-making.Here are several reasons why computer knowledge is valuable for entrepreneurs:

- **Digital Presence:** Entrepreneurs need to establish and maintain a digital presence for their businesses. This includes creating and managing websites, social media profiles, and online marketing campaigns. Computer knowledge is essential for understanding and leveraging these digital platforms effectively.
- **Communication and Collaboration:** Entrepreneurs often need to communicate and collaborate with team members, clients, and partners. Computer skills, including proficiency in email, messaging apps, and collaborative tools, enable efficient communication and coordination.
- **Data Management and Analysis:** Entrepreneurs deal with large amounts of data related to their business operations, customer interactions, and market trends. Computer skills are crucial for managing and analysing data, which can provide valuable insights for strategic decision-making.
- **E-commerce and Online Transactions:** With the growth of e-commerce, entrepreneurs need to understand online transaction systems, payment gateways, and secure online payment methods. Computer knowledge is essential for managing online sales and transactions securely.
- **Automation and Productivity Tools:** Entrepreneurs can enhance productivity by using automation tools and software. Computer skills are necessary for implementing and optimizing these tools, whether it's automating repetitive tasks, managing customer relationships, or streamlining business processes.

- **Cybersecurity Awareness:** Entrepreneurs need to be aware of cybersecurity threats and best practices to protect their businesses and customer data. Basic computer knowledge is essential for understanding potential risks and implementing security measures.
- **Adaptability and Learning:** The business landscape is dynamic, and technology evolves rapidly. Entrepreneurs with strong computer skills are better equipped to adapt to new technologies and trends. Continuous learning in the realm of technology is a valuable trait for staying competitive.
- **Tech Start-up Opportunities:** For entrepreneurs in the technology sector, computer knowledge is not just an advantage but a necessity. Understanding the technical aspects of the products or services they offer is crucial for success in tech start-ups.
- **Remote Work and Virtual Teams:** The ability to work remotely and manage virtual teams has become increasingly important. Entrepreneurs with computer skills can effectively lead teams regardless of geographical locations, leveraging online collaboration tools.
- **Problem Solving and Troubleshooting:** Computer knowledge equips entrepreneurs with problem-solving skills, enabling them to troubleshoot technical issues independently or communicate effectively with technical teams to resolve issues promptly.

Role and Importance of Entrepreneur in Economic Development

For a nation to prosper economically, entrepreneurs are essential. Economic resources by themselves won't lead to development. Dynamic businesspeople with vision, ambition, and the will to transform the economic landscape should exist. India is frequently described as "a rich country inhabited by the destitute." India has a nice climate and a wealth of natural resources. Despite these advantages, our nation is still in the early stages of development. The absence of enough innovative business owners is the primary cause of this underdevelopment. Only when a nation is able to successfully exploit its natural resources can it experience economic development.The key points that show the pivotal role played by the entrepreneurs in the economic development are as follows.

- **Capital Formation:** Capital is essential for every business. One single individual will not be able to contribute the entire capital required for a big business concern. So, the entrepreneur mobilises the small and scattered savings from the households and this will lead to capital formation.
- **Generating Employment opportunities:** The most important socio-economic problem faced by the developing countries is

unemployment. The entrepreneurs by setting up new business concerns can generate employment opportunities. Most of the entrepreneurial concerns are labour oriented. They provide large scale employment opportunities to the unemployed. Finally, this will lead to improvement in the standard of living of the people.

- **Balanced regional development:** Setting up of business concerns in the rural or under developed areas will help to achieve a balanced regional development of the nation. Small business concerns can be set up at places where raw materials and labour forces are available.
- **Reduces the concentration of economic power:** Entrepreneurship reduces the accumulation of economic power in a few hands. It ensures a wider distribution of economic power among the people.
- **Encourages the effective utilisation of capital and natural resources:** Entrepreneurs help in the effective utilisation of idle funds in the society. They can also profitably utilise the natural resources at their place of operation. In the absence of entrepreneurs these funds and resources will be kept idle.
- **Promotes Export trade:** Exports are necessary for earning foreign exchange. So, the countries follow a policy of export promotion and import substitution. Entrepreneurs setting up their business as Export Oriented Units (EOU) at Export Promotion Zones (EOZ) will help to increase the level of exports of the nation. The level of exports is one of the vital ingredients of economic development.
- **Promotes the equitable distribution of wealth, national income, and political power:** Entrepreneurship helps to achieve the socialistic objective of the nation. It helps to reduce disparity in income and wealth of the people. It creates wealth, generates employment and income, and increases the standard of living of the people.
- **Stimulates economic development:** Entrepreneurship induces backward and forward linkages and thus stimulates the process of economic development of the country.

In short, entrepreneurs are the human agents needed to mobilize capital, to exploit natural resources, to create markets, and to carry on trade. The economic progress of the USA, Japan and the European countries highlights the significance of entrepreneurship in economic development. The overall role of entrepreneurship in economic development of an economy is put as an economy is the effect for which enterprise is the cause.

Importance of Entrepreneurship Education

The value of entrepreneurship education is widely acknowledged, and it aims to give students the skills, information, and inspiration to support entrepreneurial success in a range of contexts. The development of skills or qualities that enable the realisation of opportunities is the main focus of entrepreneurship education. The development of entrepreneurship is also being used as a means of fostering abilities like taking risks and problem-solving, which support achieving personal objectives and academic success.

Since India needs to develop into a global manufacturing hub, entrepreneurship is even more important in the Indian context for increasing Indian acceptance of the "made in India" brand. In order to increase employment and speed up India's rate of growth, the current administration, led by Prime Minister Shri. Narendra Modi, is particularly eager to promote young entrepreneurs. In order to achieve this, the government is putting a premium on entrepreneurship education in order to develop a pool of knowledgeable and highly competent entrepreneurs.With the Pradhan Mantri Yuva Yojana (PMYY), which was introduced in November 2016 by the Ministry of Skill Development and Entrepreneurship (MSDE), the government intends to provide online entrepreneurship education to 15 lakh students nationwide over a five-year period through 3050 project institutes. The program's goal is to establish an ecosystem that supports entrepreneurship through entrepreneurship education and training. The GLC (Global Luxury Centre), the start-up organisations and judges of "Start-up Spirits," and the NSRCEL (NS Raghavan Centre for Entrepreneur Learning) (pmjandhanyojana.co.in)

Entrepreneurship is the capacity to put ideas into practise. It is regarded as essential to fostering innovation, competitiveness, and economic progress since it encompasses creativity, innovation, and risk-taking as well as the capacity to plan and manage projects in order to achieve goals. Developing an entrepreneurial spirit helps businesses expand and form new companies. Nevertheless, entrepreneurship abilities are advantageous whether or not a person plans to start a firm in the future. They incorporate creativity, initiative, tenacity, teamwork, understanding of risk, and a feeling of responsibility, and may be applied to both people's personal and professional lives.

Role of Government in Promoting Entrepreneurship

To promote an innovative and entrepreneurial culture inside the nation, the Indian government has implemented various policies and launched a number of programmes. India's biggest problem is creating jobs. India has enormous potential to innovate, foster entrepreneurship, and generate jobs for the benefit of the world and its own country, despite possessing a distinct and noteworthy demographic advantage. The Government of India has developed numerous new programmes and opportunities in recent years to foster innovation in a variety of fields. interacting with non-governmental organisations, investors, small and large business owners, academics, industry, and the most marginalised groups in society. The Indian government has made sure that all policy actions are focused on ensuring equal opportunity for women, realising the importance of women's economic engagement and entrepreneurship in enabling the progress and prosperity of the nation. The goal of the government is to give women more access to markets, networks, loans, and trainings so they may lead India's entrepreneurial ecosystem.

India's recent efforts at promoting entrepreneurship and innovation are:

- **Start-up India:** The Government of India encourages entrepreneurship by supporting, fostering, and assisting companies at every stage of their development through the Start-up India initiative. Numerous potential businesses have benefited from the initiative's effective head start since it was launched in January 2016. Using a comprehensive, all-encompassing strategy to support businesses, the project offers a free, four-week online learning programme and has established research parks, incubators, and startup centres all throughout the nation by building a robust network of academic and business organisations. More significantly, a "Fund of Funds" has been established to assist entrepreneurs in obtaining capital. The initiative's central goal is to create an ecosystem where start-ups can flourish and innovate without facing obstacles. To this end, various mechanisms have been put in place, including online start up recognition, the start-up India Learning Programme, facilitated patent filing, easy compliance regulations, relaxed procurement regulations, incubator support, student programmes with an innovation focus, funding support, tax benefits, and regulatory assistance.
- **Made in India:** Made in India is a project that was introduced in September 2014 with the goal of making India a global centre for design and production. It was a strong call to action for business leaders and Indian residents alike, as well as an invitation to prospective global partners and investors to modernise antiquated procedures and regulations and to consolidate data regarding prospects in the country's manufacturing industry. As a result, the business community in India, prospective partners overseas, and the general public now have more faith in India's ·
capabilities. One of the biggest initiatives in recent memory was the Make in India plan. The programme has, among other things, made sure that systems that are visible and easy to use have

replaced outdated and obstructive frameworks. Consequently, this has promoted investment, encouraged innovation, develop skills, protect intellectual property and build best-in-class manufacturing infrastructure.

- **Atal Innovation Mission (AIM):** The Government of India's initiative, known as AIM, aims to foster an innovative and entrepreneurial culture. It does this by providing a forum for the promotion of Grand Challenges, world-class Innovation Hubs, start-up companies, and other forms of self-employment, especially in technology-driven fields. Atal Tinkering Labs (ATL) are a new initiative by AIM that aim to promote imagination, creativity, and curiosity in the classroom all around India. ATLs are work areas where students can work with tools and equipment to practise applying STEM (Science, Technology, Engineering, and Math) ideas practically. Another initiative of AIM is to develop creative start-ups into scalable and long-lasting businesses by means of Atal Incubation Centres (AICs). AICs provide world class incubation facilities with appropriate physical infrastructure in terms of capital equipment and operating facilities. These incubation centres, with a presence across India, provide access to sectoral experts, business planning support, seed capital, industry partners and trainings to encourage innovative start-ups.
- **Support to Training and Employment Programme for Women (STEP):** The Ministry of Women and Child Development of the Government of India launched STEP to provide training to women who lack access to formal skill training facilities, particularly in rural areas of the country. The 30-year-old initiative's guidelines were recently revised by NITI Aayog and the Ministry of Skill Development & Entrepreneurship to better meet modern requirements. All Indian women who are older than 16 are eligible to participate in the campaign. The programme imparts skills in a variety of fields, including computer and IT services, travel and tourism, hospitality, handlooms, traditional crafts like embroidery, agriculture, gardening, and food processing.
- **Jan Dhan-Aadhaar- Mobile (JAM):** With the potential to improve the lives of millions of Indian citizens, JAM is a technical intervention that for the first time allows direct distribution of subsidies to intended beneficiaries and, in doing so, removes all intermediaries and leakages in the system. In addition to providing a crucial barrier against corruption, JAM offers accounts to all marginalised areas, enabling last-mile financial services.

- **Digital India:** In light of historically low internet penetration, the Digital India initiative aims to provide high-speed internet to all Indian households. It also aims to improve citizen participation in the digital and financial space, make India's cyberspace safer and more secure, and facilitate ease of doing business. Ultimately, Digital India hopes to achieve equity and efficiency in a nation with immense diversity by making digital resources and services available in all Indian languages. The initiative was launched with the goal of modernising the Indian economy and turning it into a knowledge economy with universal access to goods and services.
- **Biotechnology Industry Research Assistance Council (BIRAC):** The Department of Biotechnology established BIRAC, a non-profit public sector organisation, to support and enable nascent biotechnology businesses. It attempts to close the current gaps between business and academics and integrate strategic research and innovation into all biotech companies. The ultimate objective is to employ cutting edge technologies to create items that are both high-quality and reasonably priced. In order to strengthen the capabilities of the Indian biotech sector, particularly for start-ups and SME's, BIRAC has formed relationships with a number of domestic and international partners. It has also aided in a number of swift advancements in medical technology.
- **Department of Science and Technology (DST):** The DST is divided into multiple arms that work on all significant initiatives requiring the use of science and technology. By applying science and technology, the Technology Interventions for Disabled and aged, for example, offers technical solutions to address issues and enhance the quality of life for the aged in India. The ASEAN-India Science, Technology, and Innovation Cooperation, on the other hand, aims to close the development divide and improve connectivity amongst the ASEAN nations. In addition to offering fellowships to scientists and researchers from ASEAN member states working with Indian R&D/academic institutions to advance their research skills and knowledge, it promotes collaboration in science, technology, and innovation through collaborative research across sectors.
- **Trade related Entrepreneurship Assistance and Development (TREAD):** With the help of non-governmental organisations (NGOs), the TREAD programme makes loans available to eligible women in order to address the serious problem of credit access among India's impoverished women. In order to give women options to pursue non-farm pursuits, registered NGOs can assist women in obtaining credit facilities as well as possibilities for counselling and training to launch prospective businesses.

- **Pradhan Mantri Kaushal Vikas Yojana (PMKVY):** The Ministry of Skill Development & Entrepreneurship (MSDE) has launched a flagship initiative called Skill Certification, which seeks to provide youngsters with industry-relevant skills and increase their employability and chances for creating livelihoods. People who have acquired prior knowledge or abilities are also evaluated and granted certification as Recognition of Prior Learning recipients. Under this programme, the government pays all of the costs associated with assessment and training.
- **National Skill Development Mission:** The mission was initiated in July 2015 with the goal of creating cross-sector and cross-state synergies in skilled industries and initiatives. It is intended to accelerate decision-making across industries to supply skills at scale, without sacrificing quality or speed, with the goal of creating a "Skilled India." The mission's skilling activities throughout India would be guided by seven sub-missions, which were proposed in the first phase. These are: (i) Institutional Training; (ii) Infrastructure; (iii) Convergence; (iv) Trainers; (v) Overseas Employment; (vi) Sustainable Livelihoods; and (vii) Leveraging Public Infrastructure.
- **Science for Equity Empowerment and Development (SEED):** SEED seeks to give driven scientists and field personnel the chance to collaborate on location-specific, action-oriented projects for socioeconomic benefit, especially in rural areas. An attempt has been made to link national labs and other specialised S&T institutions with grassroots inventions in order to provide access to expert input and high-quality infrastructure. In order for a large portion of the population, especially the underprivileged, to benefit from technical advancements, SEED places a strong emphasis on equity in development.

Institutions set up by Central Government

- **Small industries development organization (SIDO):** Currently housed under the Ministry of Trade, Industry, and Marketing, SIDO was founded in October 1973. The Additional Secretary & Development Commissioner (Small Scale Industries) under the Ministry of Small-Scale Industries, Government of India, leads SIDO, the highest body at the national level responsible for developing policies for the growth of small-scale industries in the nation. As one of the solid cornerstones of the nation's economy, SIDO is contributing significantly to the growth of this important industry. Through its Comprehensive Plan for the Promotion of Rural Entrepreneurship, SIDO also offers further assistance.

- **Management Development Institute (MDI):** MDI is situated in Gurgaon, Haryana. Its goals are to increase managerial effectiveness in the sector. It was founded in 1973 and is supported by the Industrial Finance Corporation of India. It offers managerial development courses in a range of subjects. The curricula for officials of the IAS, IES, BHEL, ONGC, and numerous other top PSUs are also included.
- Established in 1983, the Entrepreneurship Development Institute of India (EDI) is a self-governing, non-profit organisation supported by the State Bank of India (SBI), IFCI Ltd., IDBI Bank Ltd., and ICICI Bank Ltd. Twelve state-level exclusive entrepreneurship development centres and institutes have been established with assistance from EDI. However, integrating entrepreneurship into the curricula of several schools, colleges, science and technology institutes, and management schools across multiple states was one of the rewarding accomplishments. In the global arena, EDI has received recognition and support from a number of well-known organisations, including the World Bank, Commonwealth Secretariat, UNIDO, ILO, British Council, Ford Foundation, European Union, and ASEAN Secretariat, for its efforts to promote entrepreneurship through resource sharing and training programme organisation. In addition, EDI has established Entrepreneurship Development Centres in Vietnam, Lao PDR, Myanmar, and Cambodia. It is currently in the process of establishing similar centres in Uzbekistan and five other African nations.
- **All India Small Scale Industries Board(AISSIB):** The premier advisory body established to advise the government on all matters concerning the small-scale industry is the Small Scale Industries Board (SSI Board).With a minister from the central government serving as its president and representatives from the federal government, state governments, national small industries corporations, state financial corporations, Reserve Bank of India, state banks of India, the Indian Small Industries Board, nongovernmental organisations like the Public Service Commission, and trade and industry members, it sets policies and plans for the growth of small businesses.
- **National Institution of Entrepreneurship and Small Business Development (NIESBUD), New Delhi:** It was founded by the Indian government in 1983. It is the highest authority to oversee the operations of several organisations involved in programmes for entrepreneurial development. According to the Government of India Society Act of 1860, it is a society. The institute's principal

undertakings are: To create tactics and procedures that work, To create a standardised training model curriculum, To create training materials, instruments, and guides, To hold conferences, seminars, and workshops, To assess the advantages of Enterprise Development Programmes and encourage the entrepreneurial process, To assist the government and other organisations in carrying out their plans for entrepreneur development, and To conduct research and development in the EDPs domain.

- **National Institute of Small Industries Extension Training:** It was founded in 1960 and has Hyderabad as its headquarters. The National Institute of Small Industries Extension Training's primary goals are to: Oversee and coordinate the development of curricula for small business owners, offering technical and managerial advice, Planning seminars for managers and small business owners, and Offering assistance with documentation and research.
- **National Small Industries Corporation Ltd. (NSIC):** The Central Government founded the NSIC in 1995 with the intention of supporting small businesses participating in government procurement initiatives. The company uses its marketing network to give small business items access to a sizable market. Additionally, it helps small businesses export their goods to other nations.
- **Risk Capital and Technology Finance Corporation Ltd. (RCTFC):** RCTFC was founded in 1988 with a 15-crore rupee authorised capital. The provision of venture capital for projects using advanced technological development and transfer methodologies, as well as risk capital for the extension and growth of entrepreneurial development, are the primary goals of RCTFC.
- **National Research and development corporation (NRDC):** Under the Department of Science and Industrial Research of the Indian government, NRDC was founded in 1953. Its primary goals are to: assist with technology transfer, transfer technology, build relationships with different technical institutions and gather different indigenous techniques created by them.
- **Indian Investment Centre:** The Central Government founded this independent organisation. Its primary goal is to support international collaboration between Indian and foreign entrepreneurs by giving the latter the information they require.
- **Khadi and village industries Commission (KVIC):** The Khadi and Village Industries Commission was founded in 1956 by a parliamentary act. This service organisation works to develop and promote village industries and Khadi in rural areas. Its primary

goals are to: Create jobs in rural areas, The aforementioned factors include talent enhancement, rural industrialization, technology transfer, the development of strong rural communities, Promotion of self-sufficiency among the rural populace.

- **Indian Institute of Entrepreneurship (IIE):** In 1953, the Department of Agri and Rural Industries and Small-Scale Industries founded it. It is an independent organisation with Guwahati as its headquarters. Its primary goal is to conduct research, provide training, and offer consulting services in the areas of entrepreneurship and small business.
- **Miscellaneous Organization:** In addition to above various organizations at all India level are assisting and are engaged in entrepreneur development. These include ICICI, IFCI, SIDBI, UTI, IDBI, IIBI etc.
- **National Alliance of Young Entrepreneurs (NAYE):** In association with a number of public sector banks, it has funded a variety of initiatives for entrepreneurial growth. Encouraging young entrepreneurs to investigate investment and self-employment opportunities is the primary goal of the programme. It makes training arrangements and helps them secure the funding they require. In an effort to empower women and improve their standing, NAYE also established a Women's Wing in 1975.
- **Centre for Entrepreneurial Development (CED) Ahmedabad:** The Gujrat government and state-operating public financial institutions sponsored it. It runs programmes at several centres for the growth of entrepreneurs. The following are some of the key components of the training programme: Training programmes were started following an opportunity survey, Sufficient connections were made with organisations that provided funding, manufacturing sheds, raw materials, etc., To choose the entrepreneurs, behavioural tests were administered, both theoretical and practical topics were included in training programmes, and Full-time project leader took follow up action after the training was over.
- **Institute for Entrepreneurial Development (IED):** It was set up by the IDBI in association with other financial institutions, public sector banks and the State Governments. The IEDs was set up to fulfil the entrepreneurial development needs of the industrially backward States in the country.
- **Technical Consultancy Organization (TCOs):** All India Financial Institutions and State Governments have put together a nationwide network of TCOs. These organisations were founded with the

intention of offering small business owners in particular, as well as entrepreneurs in general, a broad range of services. Among their primary duties are the following:Identifying potential industrial project, preparing project reports, feasibility reports and pre-investment status, identifying potential entrepreneurs, providing technical and administrative support, conducting techno-economic studies of the projects, conducting market research and surveys, and Rendering advice to set up laboratories and design centre.

- **Public sector banks:** Public sector banks and NAYE have partnered to offer programmes for the promotion of entrepreneurship. These banks' primary goal has been to locate prospective business owners in underdeveloped and rural areas. For instance, in the States of West Bengal and Bihar, the Punjab National Bank launched an entrepreneurial aid scheme in March 1977. In a similar vein, the Bank of India began offering entrepreneurial support in August 1972 to residents of the Union Territories of Chandigarh and Delhi as well as the States of Punjab, Rajasthan, Himachal Pradesh, and J&K.The important Forms of entrepreneurial assistance are: Identifying potential entrepreneurs, identifying viable projects, assisting in preparation of project profiles, helping in project evaluation, arranging practical training, and financing the projects.
- **Institutions set up at State Level:** There are a number of institutions establishes at state level for organizing, developing, assisting and making successful entrepreneurial development programmes. Prominent among these are: Small Industries Service Institute (SISI), State Financial Corporation (SFC), State Small Industries Corporation (SSIC), District Industries Centres (DIC), Technical Consulting Organization Ltd. (TCO), Industrial Directorates, Commercial and Cooperative Banks, State Industrial Development Corporation, Industrial Estates, State Industries Corporation.

The above-mentioned State and Central level Institutions have provided a number of concessions and facilities to promote entrepreneur development in India. They have also played an important role in balanced industrial development in the country.

NEED AND SIGNIFICANCE OF THE STUDY

The changes that happen in the Indian economy always bring modification in the educational system. It is through education one is able to become motivated self-sufficient creative and innovative educational programs are always designed in such a way that they can inculcate these values among the students and that will help them to build a successful career.The major problem faced by our country is that of widespread of unemployment and underemployment in educated youth. The percentage of students who pass out from reputed educational institutions are increasing day by day and the expenditure incurred in training engineers and diploma holders is quite high. By giving proper entrepreneurial training and guidance these persons can be groomed as entrepreneurs who can contribute for the development of our economy.

Today most of the universities are providing entrepreneurship education to the students in order to create an entrepreneurial mind set and entrepreneurial awareness among young generation. The major idea behind this is to develop an entrepreneurial attitude and behaviour in the society. In 1980's a small number of entrepreneurship course were in the US but it is growing increasingly and now entrepreneurship has become a subject offered more or less at all major universities worldwide (Politis, 2017). The reason behind this is that human resources are considered as the greatest asset to a country and for a country to become strong, the resources must be developed and nourished with proper education and training.

Apart from this, the Government of India also implemented a wide variety of schemes and programs in order to enhance entrepreneurial attitudeamong the youth. The implementation of entrepreneurship education to under graduate level can be considered as one of the strategies adopted by our government to create an entrepreneurial culture among the students.The curriculum of commerce education is mainly focused on vocational aim of education and implementing entrepreneurial programmes in commerce education helps to create an entrepreneurial attitude among students. It is assumed that the aim of entrepreneurship development programme is to motivate a child in developing a career that enables them to explore the opportunities as well as setting up there on Enterprises.So, it is essential to analyse the entrepreneurial skills among B. Com students.

STATEMENT OF THE PROBLEM

One of the curriculum objectives of commerce education is to prepare a student for a career in business enterprise of his/her own initiative. For ensuring the achievement of this objective a student must get as much as experience for exhibiting or realizing his traits and skills. The entrepreneurial traits are considered essential for an individual, particularly for commerce students to function an economic activity at their own initiative as well as to take part in the career opportunities afford by the commerce education. This study focuses to analyse the entrepreneurial traits among undergraduate commerce students. Hence the present study is entitled as "Analysis of Entrepreneurial traits among B. Com Students".

OPERATIONAL DEFINITION OF KEY TERMS

- **Entrepreneurial Traits:** Typical characteristics, abilities and thought patterns associated with successful entrepreneurs. In the present study, it means analysing the entrepreneurial characteristics, abilities and thought patterns of B. Com students to become a successful entrepreneur.
- **B. Com Students:** Com or Bachelor of Commerce course is a three-year undergraduate course recognised by the University Grants Commission (UGC). For this present study B.Com students means select the sample students consist of 200 students from different colleges of Kottayam and Idukki districts.

OBJECTIVES OF THE STUDY

- To analyse the level of entrepreneurial traits among B. Com students
- To analyse the entrepreneurial traits among B. Com students on the basis of gender
- To analyse the entrepreneurial traits among B. Com students on the basis of type of institution
- To analyse the entrepreneurial traits among B. Com students on the basis of locality

HYPOTHESIS OF THE STUDY

- The level of entrepreneurial traits among B. Com students are poor
- There is no significant difference in the entrepreneurial traits among B.Com students on the basis of gender
- There is no significant difference in the entrepreneurial traits among B.Com students on the basis of type of institution
- There is no significant difference in the entrepreneurial traits among B.Com students on the basis of locality

METHODOLOGY OF THE STUDY

In the present study, normative survey method was employed by the investigator. Simple random sampling technique was used in this study. By giving sufficient weightage to the factors like gender, type of institution, locality of the institution, a sample of 200 B. Com students from 2 districts of Kerala were selected for the study.

Tools used: In the present study, the researcher used the following tool. To analyse the entrepreneurial trait among B. Com students, the researcher used an assessment scale titled "Entrepreneurial trait assessment scale" developed by Madhusoodhanan & Thamarasseri (2022). The tool consists 60 items under 12 dimensions and each dimension consist of 5 items. The dimensions are mentioned below:

(a) Conceptual aspect
(b) Technical aspect
(c) Human relation aspect
(d) Communication aspect
(e) Decision- making aspect.
(f) Managerial aspect
(g) Time management aspect
(h) Stress management aspect
(i) Personality & individual aspect
(j) Pioneering/Risk taking aspect
(k) Unification & Organization aspect
(l) Computer knowledge aspect

Population: The population of the study consist of B. Com students in the various colleges and other higher education institutions.

Sample: A sample is the representative proportion of the population. The sample for the study consists of 200 commerce graduate students at various colleges from Kottayam and Idukki districts. Due representation is given to relevant demographic variables, such as gender, locale of the institution and type of management of the institution.

SCOPE OF THE STUDY

The purpose of the present study is to analyse the entrepreneurial traits among commerce students at undergraduate level. The study was conducted on a representative sample of 200 students from four colleges of Kottayam and Idukki district. This study may be helpful to find out the conceptual, technical, human relation, communication, decision-making, managerial, time management, stress management, personality & individual, pioneering/risk taking, unification & organization and computer knowledge aspect that an individual may possess to become an entrepreneur. All these aspects were investigated with respect to the demographic variables. The tools constructed for the present study are valid and reliable. Findings of this study will help to understand the entrepreneurial trait of commerce students at undergraduate level.

It is expected that the findings of the study may be helpful to the educational policy makers, educational administrators, teachers, parents and all those who is concerned with generating employment opportunities for the benefit of each and every student. This study will also help the teachers and the students to focus their attention to develop entrepreneurial traits and entrepreneurial attitude. The study may also provide a chance to the students to identify their core traits and thereby they can improve those traits. The findings of the study may also useful for the teachers to reframe the method of teaching.

LIMITATIONS OF THE STUDY

- The sample size is little less due to administrative reason and hence the result of the study cannot be taken as universal
- The study is delimited to commerce graduate students only
- Due to non – availability of time, only one tool is used in the study
- Certain respondents were reluctant in providing information, thus hampering the result and also lack of accurate information from the students.

ORGANISATION OF THE REPORT

Every research report must be clearly organised so as to help the users for further reference. Normally a research report comprises three main sections:Preliminaries, Main body andReference section. The present report is organised in the following way.

- **Preliminaries:** This section includes the title page, acknowledgement, Table of Contents, list of tables, list of figures, list of appendices etc.
- **Main body:** The main body of the thesis is organised in five chapters as follows.
  - **Chapter 1:** Introduction: This chapter contains Background of the study, Need and significance of the study, Statement of the problem, Operational definition of the key terms, Hypothesis of the study, Objectives of the study, Methodology in brief, Limitations of the study, and Scope of the study.
  - **Chapter 2:** Review of related literature: This chapter contains review of related literature.
  - **Chapter 3:** Methodology: This chapter gives a detailed description of the method adopted, variables of the study, population and sample selected for the study, method adopted for the study, tools and techniques, data collection procedure, consolidation of data, statistical techniques used for the study.
  - **Chapter 4:** Analysis and Interpretation of the Collected Data: This chapter is concerned with the analysis of the data and interpretations of analysis made in accordance with the objectives and hypothesis formulated.

  - **Chapter 5:** Summary, conclusion, and suggestions: This chapter presents summary of the study, major findings, conclusion based on the findings, educational implications of the study and suggestions for further research.
- **Reference Section:** This section includes reference of the cited sources. It will be helpful for further researchers.
- **Appendices:** It comprises the details of trait assessment scale.

Review of the Related Literature

INTRODUCTION

The process of gathering, choosing, and reading books, journals, papers, abstracts, and other reference materials constitutes a review of related literature. A systematic explicit and reproducible approach for locating, analysing, and interpreting the body of recorded work created by researchers and practitioners is known as a literature review. Best (1986) asserts that a cursory review of prior studies and the writings of reputable specialists shows that the researcher is first familiar with what is known and with what is yet unknown and untested. The relevant literature demonstrates where to find important concepts, theories, and hypotheses as well as useful data regarding issues, assessments of contemporary methods, and practical studies. Literature review is an assessment of a body of research that addresses and identify what is already known about an area of study.

A literature review is a report that evaluates the data from the literature in relation to particular fields of research. If addressed in an orderly fashion, the study of related material can be completed almost painlessly and is just as significant as any other steps in the research process. The methodical identification, location, and analysis of papers providing data relevant to the study subject constitute the review of related literature. A review of the literature has practical applications in research; information from the literature is used to analyse the importance of the topic, construct the research design, connect the study's findings to existing knowledge, and propose additional investigation.

In writing the literature review, the purpose is to convey to the reader what knowledge and ideas established on a topic, and what their strengths and weaknesses are. The literature review must be defined by a guiding concept (e.g., research objective, the problem or issues are discussing or argumentative thesis). It is not just a descriptive list of the material available, or a set of summaries.

The source of information has been classified as direct and indirect sources. In the field of education, the direct sources of information are available in the form of education literature which includes educational journals, Books, Year books and bulletins, Dissertation, Thesis and Government publication.

The indirect sources are available in the form of Encyclopaedia of Education, Education Indexes, Education abstracts, Directories and bibliographies, Bibliographical references, Quotation sources, and Miscellaneous sources.

A literature review is a comprehensive summary of previous research on a topic. The literature review surveys scholarly articles, books, and other sources relevant to a particular area of research. The review should enumerate, describe, summarize, objectively evaluate and clarify the previous research. It should give a theoretical base for the research and help the researcher to determine the nature of the research. The literature review acknowledges the work of previous researchers, and in so doing, assures the reader that your work has been well conceived. It is assumed that by mentioning a previous work in the field of study, that the author has read, evaluated, and assimilated that work into the work at hand.

According to Cooper (1988) a literature review uses of its database reports of primary or original scholarship and does not report new primary scholarship itself. The primary reports used in the literature maybe verbal, but in the last majority of cases reports are written documents. The types of scholarship may be empirical, theoretical, critical or analytic, or methodological in nature. Second literature review seeks to describe summaries, evaluate, clarify and/or integrate the content of primary report.

The review of related literature enables the researcher to define the limits of the field of research. It is a help the researcher to de limit and define his/her problem. The knowledge of related literature brings the research up to date on the work which others have done and thus to state the object is clearly and concisely.

The findings of past research that have been conducted in the field of the current study are the main focus of the review of the literature. It looks at potential directions for current and upcoming study on the topic. In actuality, it wasn't until the late 1950s that entrepreneurship became a topic of scholarly discussion. Since then, academics and academicians in India and abroad have conducted several research studies on various aspects of the study. It contains several articles, working papers, and research materials that span a wide range of topics. Linking the current study with the past is possible if an open and sincere assessment of the literature is made to guarantee that the research gaps exposed by earlier attempts are identified. The research that has been reviewed in relation to this work are listed below in chronological sequence.

Bhuyan & Manjib (2021) conducted a study on the topic "Entrepreneurial Intent assessment among university students in Uttarakhand region". The study made an effort to determine and investigate the effects of environmental and motivational elements on university students in order to objectively prove the existence of Entrepreneurial Intention (EI). From the viewpoint of students, the study thoroughly examined the relationship between EI and its associated constructs, which could be crucial in determining an entrepreneur's success or failure. To explore the students' intentions toward entrepreneurship, five research questions were created, and to evaluate them, a measurement approach based on the Theory of Planned Behaviour was used. The study's conclusions show that TPB is a reliable method for conducting behavioural research and that it is the best predictor of entrepreneurship intention (EI).

Muhammed (2020) conducted a study on the topic "Effectiveness of Entrepreneurship Skill Development Programme Conducted by Micro Small Medium Enterprises Development Institute of Kerala. This study aims to analyse and evaluate the effectiveness of Entrepreneurship Skill Development Programme conducted by MSME, Kerala for the benefit of weaker section of the society.

In their study, **Varalakshmi, Srivani, and Rao (2019)** sought to understand how young people view entrepreneurship. The study's main goal was to assess young people's attitudes about entrepreneurship. There are 100 respondents from various academic fields and professions made up the sample size. They were chosen by use of a stratified random sampling procedure. The findings demonstrate that regardless of educational background, men and women see entrepreneurship prospects similarly. The youth's propensity for entrepreneurship is influenced by factors like economic standing, employment status, and annual income. It is necessary to raise awareness of business opportunities, financial options, government incentives, corporate and business rules, etc.

Ish and Hashim (2018) conducted a study to examine the significance of entrepreneurial skills and their influence on entrepreneurial career option. A total of 505 questionnaires were delivered to Nigerian polytechnic students as part of a quantitative approach. The stratified random sampling approach was used to select a sample of 361 pupils. The study used a quantitative research methodology and social science investigations. The study's findings show that know-who and know-when skills have a strong favourable impact on choosing an entrepreneurial career.

Ashoka and Abrishami (2018) conducted a study to demonstrate the effectiveness of SIDBI's support for MSMEs' entrepreneurial endeavours. Describing the application of the demographic advantage to ensure that individuals in India have access to employment prospects despite having less education and skills. Their study demonstrates how the two groups overcame early obstacles to assist the growth of entrepreneurship through the provision of mentorship services, market connections, loan access, networking, and business space, among other things. Through initiatives like Start-up India, Ease of Doing Business, stand up India, MUDRA, and the Atal Innovation Mission, the government also supports entrepreneurs.

Sree (2018) talked about the importance of and trends in Indian entrepreneurship in her study. The study's main objective was to examine the barriers and opportunities that encourage people to launch new businesses as well as the difficult issues that hinder their success. It was an exploratory study with 172 participants. Unstructured questionnaires were created with questions about preferences, motivating factors, reasons why people didn't choose entrepreneurship, and other similar topics. Difficulties experienced by business owners. A rise in entrepreneurship results in a decline in the unemployment rate, technical independence, and foreign currency flows. According to the report, becoming wealthy quickly, creating jobs for others, and having a sense of style or ambition are the main motivations for selecting entrepreneurship as a career. Lack of financial and familial support, as well as the uncertainty of business success, were the main factors in people opting not to pursue entrepreneurship as a career.

Rabi (2018) in a study on feminist theory and its impact on female entrepreneur's growth intentions, tried to explore the gender differences among entrepreneurs in the success of their ventures. Numerous studies on the subject have indicated that entrepreneurs have different goals for growing their companies, and that men are more successful than women in doing so. This phenomenon has been highlighted in numerous earlier studies, and it can be shown that the majority of these studies are carried out in industrialised nations. Feminist perspective theories, according to many academics, are required to provide more in-depth knowledge of the subject. This essay's goal is to analyse the studies on female entrepreneurs' growth objectives and offer alternate viewpoints by incorporating feminist theories. In order to evaluate the growth objectives in company, the scholar has conducted a thorough examination of the literature on female entrepreneurship. The study applies a desk research approach for collecting the data. The study recommends certain policy measures to support women entrepreneurs to overcome the inertia of low growth aspirations.

Reyad and Badawi (2018) conducted a study in Arab region business schools to find out the relationship of start-ups career of accounting students and their cognitive skills. Communication skills, problem solving skills and logical thinking are included in the cognitive skills. The study showed that the course of entrepreneurship and starting-up a business, entrepreneurship education of cognitive skills can be well trained and considered as a winning factor.

Ahmed, Pahi, Mozammel, and Umrani (2018) addressed the intention toward entrepreneurship. Three hundred eighty-eighty female management students from five top private universities participated in the study in Kuala Lampur. They looked into the contribution of entrepreneurial self-efficacy to entrepreneurial intention. Higher self-efficacy among female students is associated with increased entrepreneurial intent. The respondents who expressed greater self-confidence in their capacity to learn new things and apply that knowledge expressed a desire to take on business ventures. According to the research, those who believe they can succeed as business owners are more likely to be inspired to increase their propensity for entrepreneurship. Respondents who are eager to take on difficulties and take chances express their interest in inclination. The female pupils' ability to take risks was encouraged by entrepreneurial education. Those who have a basic understanding of entrepreneurship are said to be able to face problems and capable of doing so with good intentions.

Herath & Amarawansha (2018) in their research article. The study's major goal was to discover the issues and the influences that lead people to change their minds about becoming entrepreneurs. For the study, 100 undergraduates who studied entrepreneurship were used as the sample. In this investigation, convenient sampling was employed. The findings indicated that students' negative attitudes regarding entrepreneurship due to a lack of actual business knowledge, experience garnered from their parents' businesses, and friends' and relatives' job aspirations caused them to rethink beginning a career in business. As a result, those involved in fostering entrepreneurial abilities among groups like the government institutions that grow in people's minds, including educational institutions. Different seminars should be given in media platforms like radio and television to incorporate these abilities. Additionally, they can hold competitions and workshops on business growth to provide participants real-world experience and reduce customer mistrust of newly created ventures.

Ireogbu (2017) conducted a study in postgraduate early childhood education students to ascertain their attitude towards entrepreneurial skills training sessions in early childhood education sector. This study is a descriptive research project that uses exploratory exercises to teach early childhood education students—a purposeful sample of 38 higher degree candidates—entrepreneurial capabilities. The sample consisted of 20 female and 18 male students enrolled in early childhood education academic programmes. The Entrepreneurial Skills Attitude Scale was one of the tools the investigator utilised (ESAS). According to survey results, 95% of students like learning entrepreneurial skills, and 87% plan to start their own early childhood education programmes after graduation. 53 percent of graduates wanted to work in the creation of children's books, while 84 percent preferred to be self-employed after graduation. Gender and age did not significantly influence trainee opinions.

Mbanefo and Eboka (2017) carryout a study to examine the innovative and entrepreneurial skills needed in basic science education for job creation and the teaching strategies required. The study was conducted in Nigeria with a population of 441 principals and 4340 basic science teachers. Questionnaire was used for data collection. The findings revealed that a lot of skills were needed in science education for job creation, the teachers were required to use practically oriented methods in teaching the students, and a lot of factors posed challenges to the acquisition of entrepreneurial skills in basic science education.

Sudarwati (2017) conducted a study to improve student's entrepreneurial skills, mostly to their managerial aspects through developing a complete practical module. The study adopted a research and development approach and a design-based research methodology. Data collection and analysis were done using a design-based methodology. The following steps were conducted for the research: problem identification, objective framing, product design and development, product inspection and testing, result evaluation, and result communicating. The study's findings suggest that the integrated entrepreneurship module was ultimately successful in improving students' capacity to both understand and apply concepts related to managerial and entrepreneurial skills.

Osakede, Lawanson & Sobowale (2017) in their study mentioned that Entrepreneurial interest among the youth population is a panacea for unemployment especially due to high turnout of educated individuals in the labour force. In this paper the factors that determine entrepreneurship interest among the youth population in Nigeria were discussed. The University of Ibadan was used as a case study. The level of entrepreneurial involvement and gender variations, as well as empirical findings on whether it affects academic success, were discussed. The factors that affect entrepreneurship interest and interference with academic achievement, respectively, were examined using the logit and multinomial logit models.

Descriptive statistics and the t-test were used to examine the level of involvement and determine whether there is a statistically significant difference between genders. According to the findings, I subjective norm, perceived behavioural control, and family business background strongly influence students' interest in entrepreneurship; (ii) engaging in entrepreneurial activity has no significant impact on students' academic achievement. In addition, findings also suggest relatively low entrepreneurial engagement among students with significant differences across gender.

Hmedat, Ali, & Muthuraman (2017) examined the entrepreneurial intents and initiatives of management students. They made the point that higher education contributes to the development of the country. Most management students were eager to start their own business in order to pursue a profession. There are 100 students were chosen at random to make up the sample size. The majority of respondents report not having any entrepreneurial training. The most influential people were their families, teachers, successful businesspeople, and their desire to start their own company. The majority of students are interested in starting their own businesses in the manufacturing, service, and trading sectors.

Khursheed (2017) examined how Central University of Punjab students perceived their own entrepreneurship potential. There were 40 students in the sample, chosen through purposive sampling, and both male and female students were included. This study aims to evaluate the entrepreneurial intents of MBA and M.Phil./MS programme students from the previous academic year. The results demonstrate that the majority of students believe that someone who possesses qualities like self-assurance, self-efficacy, and self-control can launch a new firm. Few students said that having a lack of professional skills and confidence makes it difficult to start your own business. Several respondents said they would never take a risk because they were afraid of failing and suffering financial loss.

Hajam and Ali (2017) conducted a study to know the role of innovative entrepreneurship in economic development of G20 countries of the world and found that the crucial factor for the success of growth of these economies are the result of the contribution given by entrepreneurial ventures which are innovative. By a survey conducted in 2013 on 1500 entrepreneurs across the entire G20 countries, the researchers tried to find out the barriers for the development of entrepreneurs in these countries. The authors found close interrelationship between entrepreneurship, innovation and economic development and the governments of these nations should provide a proper entrepreneurial ecosystem to support its growth.

Durai & Thavaraj (2017) in this study an attempt was taken by the researchers to identify the level of attitude towards entrepreneurship among the post graduate business studies students. In Dindigul district, four colleges were randomly chosen for the study through lot and the final year post graduate students studying M.B.A., M.Com., M. Com (C.A.), M.A. (Economics), M.F.T form the population of the study. The sample design adopted for the study is convenience sampling. The sample size was arbitrarily chosen as 200. Structured questionnaire was used to collect primary data. The findings of the study reveal that the female students are having more inclination towards starting their own business when compared with the male students of business studies.

Mario, Madrid and Garcia (2016) conducted a study to find out how entrepreneurial skill and Socio-cultural factors affect secondary education students' propensity towards entrepreneurial options in their future career. Secondary education students in the Murcia Region were the sample of the study. The tool used for the study was questionnaire. The result of the study found out that both the entrepreneurial skill and socio-cultural factors positively affect entrepreneurial intention of secondary school students. Creativity, proactivity, and risk taking and those students whose role model is an entrepreneur promote entrepreneurial career.

Karim & Venkataiah (2016) conducted a study on Comparative research on attitudes towards entrepreneurship. They made the case that entrepreneurship contributes more to the nation's economic expansion. They wanted to talk about how the students felt about starting new businesses and being entrepreneurs. As samples, the students enrolled in UG and PG programmes in the Andhra Pradeshian district of Chittoor were chosen. The outcome demonstrates that students have a favourable impression of the desirability of new ventures and a desire to found a new company. The majority of students believe that today, more than in years past, it is challenging to launch a new firm.

Rathna. C, et al., (2016) made an empirical analysis on factors that play a role of motivator in enhancing the aspect of entrepreneurship among women, with special reference to Thanjavur district. This study also focuses attention on the challenges faced by women in the pursuit of entrepreneurship. Descriptive research design was used for this study. The primary data was collected from 400 samples from rural and urban areas of Thanjavur district using a structured questionnaire with the help of survey and snow ball sampling method and study has used Rotated Component Matrix to factorise the important motivational factors. The outcome of the Rotated Component Matrix shows that the extraction procedure was applied to the twelve variables before the five factors were examined. The first indicator is that women have joined this venture as a pastime activity and are still working at home. The survey also showed that they started these business endeavours in order to gain financial independence and raise their social standing. The outcome also indicated that difficult market conditions and strict legal and regulatory requirements have been more difficult than other issues. Finally, the outcome demonstrates that women entrepreneurs have had several personal difficulties as a result of knowledge gaps and an unbalanced balance between work and family life.

Sankar & Sutha (2016) conducted a study to examine the college students' Mind-set and intentions toward entrepreneurship. Entrepreneurship is considered as engine of economic growth. That plays a great role in the economic growth and development of the country, more so in a rapidly developing country like India. Entrepreneurship development today has assumed great significance as it is a key to economic development. Greater employment possibilities, an increase in per capita income, a higher standard of living, and balanced regional development are the fruits of industrial development, which is sown by entrepreneurs. The current research makes an effort to review and analyse the empirical studies conducted to determine college students' entrepreneurial intentions and the factors influencing their decision to pursue entrepreneurship. The study's key findings include that household income, age, and gender of entrepreneurs as well as their sociodemographic traits, particularly their level of education, are all substantially connected with their motivations for entrepreneurship. Particularly, the overlap between the entrepreneur's business and previous employment, the availability of role models, whether the business was started alone or with others, and the industry sector show distinct associations between the entrepreneur's personal situation at the time of business start-up and motivations.

Yong (2016), examines and analysed topic that whether entrepreneurship can promote local employment and wage structure and tries to find out what is the degree of relationship between these variables. In this study, two different sets of variables are used such as homestead exemption levels in bankruptcy laws and the share of metropolitan statistical area overlaying aquifers. The researcher used two sets of instrument variables to examine the relationship and found that the estimates are similar for both the instruments. It was found that a 10% increase in the formation of small business units enhanced the employment by 1.3% to 2.2% and the payroll expenses by 2.4% to 4% in the metropolitan areas of the country.

Najafabadi, Zamani and Mirdamadi (2016) undertook research to determine the connections between entrepreneurial goals, self-efficacy, attitudes toward entrepreneurship, psychological attributes, social norms, and perceived desirability. In order to pinpoint this, the authors turned to Shapiro's entrepreneurial event model and Ajzen's theory of planned behaviour. The study covers the predisposing factors for entrepreneurial intention in agriculture students as well. Data collecting involved using a survey method. According to the study, entrepreneurial competence (63%), self-efficacy (44%), attitude toward entrepreneurship (38%), psychological qualities (11%), and societal norms (0.08%) were the latent variables that had the greatest impact on entrepreneurial intention.

Amritha (2016) in her study on entrepreneurship and economic development, states that entrepreneurs function as a trigger to spark the momentum of economic activities through innovative decisions. The entrepreneurial talents play a prominent role not only in the development of industrialization but all other sectors of the economy, including the farm sector also. The author compares the entrepreneurial initiative as a sort of gambling the success of which is based on the right decisions and right efforts in right time. The role played by the entrepreneur cannot be generalized across all sectors of the economy as well as in between the economies of the world as it varies from economy to economy depending on the availability of material resources, proper industrial environment and support from the political system. The author states that the entrepreneurial ventures 46 lead to a vicious circle of progress in the economy by unleashing chain of events such as introduction of new products, which results in new employment, more income, more demand and more expansion of business ventures.

Vorley and Williams (2016) done a study to check the effectiveness of smartphone apps in fostering effectual thinking and also consider the powerful development of entrepreneurial ideas and the related change in entrepreneurial support and perceived entrepreneurial skills of student. Sample consisted of undergraduate management students who had no previous enterprise education. Results of the study shows that smart phone-based learning increased the development of entrepreneurial ideas, as well as increasing entrepreneurial confidence and entrepreneurial skill of the participants.

Renugadevi & Antony (2016) examine the entrepreneurial traits among colleges students in Madurai city. Objectives of the study is to have a study about traits of college students to start business, to examine general attitudes of students towards entrepreneurship and to analyse the problems faced by students for entering in to entrepreneurship "Sampling method, which is used in this study, is random sampling – when population elements are selected for inclusion in the sample based on the case of access. Major findings of the study highlight that 86% of the respondents are interested in starting business after the completion of their studies and Majority of the respondents 68% say that current curriculum is helpful in entrepreneurship. This study suggests that through adapting curriculum and implementing practical initiative, students can be given the opportunity to develop these skills.

In his study, **Majeed (2016)** looked into college students' awareness of and propensity for entrepreneurship. The study explores their level of awareness, their skill set, and their issues. agreed upon and tactics for fostering entrepreneurship adopted. There are 150 college students made up the sample size. Reading, lectures, and media all helped the pupils become informed. All students at the college must receive entrepreneurship education. According to the survey, having strong management, writing, and communication abilities was crucial for success as an entrepreneur. According to the study, practical instruction is required. It is necessary to redesign the curriculum and syllabus.

Amubode & Goriola (2015) conducted a study to assess the Entrepreneurial Personality Trait of final year students of clothing, textile and interior decoration prior to business start – up and their future plan after graduation. All the final year students were used for the study. Questionnaire was used to gather the data which was designed using Granger and Sterling Personal Assessment Scale. The results show that about one-third (32.14%) of the students have plan to be self-employed after graduation, 14.29% want to travel abroad, 28.57% want to further their academic career while 25% want to secure job in either private or public sector. the average personality score of the students is 74.06 (Mid-to-Lower range) indicating that the students need to spend more time to develop their entrepreneurial skills so as to succeed in a socio-economic challenging environment.

Pulka et al., (2015) in their study entitled "The Effects of Entrepreneurship Education on University Students' Attitude and Entrepreneurial Intention" had investigated the relationship that exists between offering entrepreneurship education course and students' intention to become entrepreneurs in selected universities in north east Nigeria. The population of the study were all undergraduate students from five selected universities in north east Nigeria. Purposive sampling was used in selecting the five universities, while simple random sampling was used in selecting four faculties and respondents from each university. The results showed that the students agreed that there is positive relationship between offering entrepreneurship education and their intention to become entrepreneurs. The Pearson correlation results also showed that, there is positive relationship between offering entrepreneurship education course and students' intention to become entrepreneurs.

Rengamani & Ramachandran (2015) analysed the role of quality entrepreneurship education and training, in identifying and nurturing this entrepreneurial potential among youth is becoming apparent to students, policy makers, and educators. Entrepreneurial development is a complex phenomenon and such process is the crystallization of social milieu from which a person comes, family imbibed personal attitudes, caste system, educational level, parental income, occupation and so on. Besides, educational institutions could play a positive role in motivating the students to venture into self-employment. In the above backdrop, this study on Entrepreneurial spirit among students, has been undertaken to identity the reasons for choosing entrepreneurship as a career and to examine the influence of various factors on students' preference towards entrepreneurship.

Kumar (2015) has studied on the entrepreneurial traits of college students in arts and science colleges in Thoothukudi District of Tamil Nadu. Proportionate stratified random sampling technique has been used for this study. It reveals that, with reference to the entrepreneurial traits for hard work, Risk-taking, Self-confidence, Information seeking, Planning, foresight and problem solving and Leadership were found to be non-significant. The corresponding t-values are not significant at 5% level. Hence the null hypothesis is accepted. With reference to the entrepreneurial traits of Decision making, it is found that there is significant difference among the Arts and science students of the respondents.

The corresponding t-values are significant at 5% level. Hence the null hypothesis is rejected.

Setiadi & Puspitasari (2014) in their study entitled "Empirical study of Entrepreneurial Attitudes and Intentions among Indonesian Business Students" had found that Indonesian business students are aware of the competencies and the qualities strongly associated with entrepreneurial success. Specifically, they have favourable views on entrepreneurs and entrepreneurship in terms of their impact to society. Interesting finding showed that entrepreneurial intentions are not solely determined by the possession of what are believed to be entrepreneurial qualities. These are jointly influenced by several factors including social factors, value system, self-efficacy, and perceptions.

Hattab (2014) in his study on undergraduate students in their last year in a private Egyptian university from three faculties, found positive relationship between entrepreneurship education and intentions. The findings suggest positive relationship between entrepreneurship education and intentions and perceived desirability while no relation existed with perceived feasibility or self-efficacy. Given the significance and importance of entrepreneurship, it is desirable to reform the educational system to encourage creativity and innovativeness of students and delivery pedagogy in a way to encourage entrepreneurial personality development including risk-taking, need for achievement, ardent desire to succeed and alertness.

Ramos (2014) studied on Entrepreneurial Intention among Business Students in Batangas State University based on their entrepreneurial capabilities and skills. The study revealed that majority of the respondents have no family business, belongs to middle income group and management major students. Further, it was found out that most of the students agreed that they possess entrepreneurial intentions, skills and capabilities. It was also found out that entrepreneurial intention is not affected by the profile variables. It only shows that the entrepreneurial intention of the students is independent with that of their profile variables.

Soleimanpour, Hosseini & Farzam (2014) in their study aimed to study the relationship between entrepreneurial characteristics and students' academic achievement at Islamic Azad University. This was applied research with descriptive correlation method. Statistical population comprised of all students studying at the Varamin-Pishva branch of Islamic Azad University in 2013. The sample of the study was 175 students selected through stratified sampling. Questionnaire was used as a tool for data collection. The results showed that the university studied students had a positive and significant relationship with perseverance and creativity at the 95% level and had a positive and significant relationship with need for achievement and locus of control at the 99% level.

Sutanto & Eliyana (2014) in their study aimed to find out the relationship between achievement motivation and attitude, attitude and entrepreneurial characteristics, and achievement motivation and entrepreneurial characteristics of the students. Partial Least Square by using path analysis was the method used in this research. The sample of this study was 69 teams of students who received funding through the business competition held in Airlangga University. Questionnaire was used as a research instrument. The results obtained from this study showed that there were significant relationships between achievement motivation and attitude, attitude and entrepreneurial characteristics, and achievement motivation and entrepreneurial characteristics of the students.

Kuttim et al., (2014) identified the content of university entrepreneurship education and its impact for students' entrepreneurial intentions. The study design used was cross-sectional study and the sample consisted of the students from 17 European countries that have been grouped for the purpose of analysis by the level of economic development into two country groups: efficiency-driven and innovation-driven economies. Frequencies and binary logistic regression were used to analyse the impact of different factors, including participation in entrepreneurship education, for entrepreneurial intentions. Results indicate that what is offered is not necessarily the most demanded in entrepreneurship education as lectures and seminars are provided more, but networking and coaching activities are expected more by the students. Participation in entrepreneurship education was found to exert positive impact on entrepreneurial intentions.

Lans (2014) analysed sustainable entrepreneurs, i.e., those who proactively facilitate latent demands for sustainable development, are now in higher demand than ever before. Higher education can play an important role in laying the foundation for these sustainable entrepreneurs. Traditionally, educational scholars focus either on the issue of education for sustainability or on entrepreneurship education. There is little work which explores and/or crosses the boundaries between these two disciplines, let alone work in which an effort is made to integrate these perspectives. In this article, a competence approach was taken as a first step to link the worlds of education for entrepreneurship and for sustainability because we postulate that both, apparently different, worlds can reinforce each other. Based on a literature review, focus group discussions with teachers in higher education and a structured questionnaire among students, a set of clear, distinct competencies was developed, providing stepping stones for monitoring students' sustainable entrepreneurship development in school-based environments.

Shah & Ali (2013) in their study entitled "Investigating Attitudes and Intentions among Potential Entrepreneurs of a Developing Country: A Conceptual Approach" had investigated the impact of entrepreneurship on education has been recognized as one of the fundamental factors that help youths to understand and foster an entrepreneurial attitude. Due to the influence, education could have on the attitudes and aspirations of youth and there is a need to understand how to develop and nurture potential entrepreneurs even while they are still students. The purpose of this study is to investigate the attitudes and intentions of individuals towards entrepreneurship. Researcher has reviewed large amount of literature and based on research gap developed a conceptual framework in which entrepreneurship intention has been directly connected with the variables such as attitudes towards the behaviour, subjective norms and perceived behavioural control and through attitudinal variables like achievement, self-esteem, personal control and innovation. This study may be recognized as one of the vital for the youths to understand and foster an entrepreneurial because due to over population, technological advancement and saturation in government employment, individuals may develop their attitudes and behaviours towards entrepreneurship education programmes. The significance of this study is that before studying entrepreneurship courses students are intended to get job in private or governmental institution but after studying the courses of entrepreneurship their mind might be diverted towards starting their own business because targeted entrepreneurial education programmes may affect to individuals' attitudes and intention. This piece of research might inspire further research work to course developers for higher educational institutions and may also support to those students who can opt for new business after completion of their studies.

Yanya et al., (2013) and other researchers have looked into the advantages of operating an entrepreneurial venture. According to this study, as the number of entrepreneurial endeavours rises, so does per capita and overall income. The growth in businesses is not significantly correlated with a reduction in poverty or an increase in the income of the poor. In addition, a study on entrepreneurs found that men are superior to women at spotting business opportunities. For instance, Dahalan et al. (2013) revealed that men are more active than women in spotting business opportunities and engaging in commercial activities. Women are less mobile to engage in entrepreneurship since they are more tied to traditions and norms. It will be also difficult for women to escape from the same which act as a barrier for entrepreneurship.

Chaudhari (2013) made an attempt to study entrepreneurial trait among various course students. It has notified some important qualities enlisted by students essential for successful entrepreneurs. Furthermore, it has studied the role of education institutes in upgrading these qualities. This study shows that the entrepreneurial motive among the respondents is very low. The reason behind this scenario is mostly due to lack of technical knowledge, unwillingness to take risk and inferior personality. The effort must be made to incorporate some leadership qualities among student. The course curriculum must be designed in a way as to give technical knowledge to students. The education institutions on the other hand must arrange the guest lecture of local entrepreneur for their students. It was suggested that arranging these lectures will help student to overcome the problems faced by them in the effort of becoming an entrepreneur.

Nkiruka et al., (2013) in their study sought to find out from the perceptions of the undergraduate students, the ICT and entrepreneurial competences needed for wealth creation. The study was carried out in Enugu State of Nigeria. The population of the study comprised of approximately 3000 final year students of University of Nigeria Nsukka and Enugu State University of Technology Enugu. Based on the findings of the study the following conclusions and recommendations among others were drawn. The study revealed that school administrators had to organize workshops intermittently, inviting resource persons who were experts in different field of study to acquaint the students with practical skills that would help them to be functional in a specific area of interest. Widening of the scope of entrepreneurial curriculum to accommodate many special areas so as to allow students' choice of choosing needed competencies according to need and interest. Students should be allowed to select entrepreneurial skills as they were interested in and should be helped to acquaint the skills through effective planning, implementation and internalization of such skills.

Zaman (2013) aims to explore the entrepreneurship profile of the Pakistan university students (Peshawar region) and evaluates their entrepreneurial inclination by making comparison with non-entrepreneurially inclined students. In this study the entrepreneurial profile of the students is constituted by six traits namely need for achievement, innovativeness, focus of control, risk taking propensity, tolerance for ambiguity, self-confidence. The results showed that except for tolerance for ambiguity and self-confidence all entrepreneurial traits are found to be higher in entrepreneurially inclined students as compared to non – inclined students. This study probes entrepreneurial characteristic providing a clear understanding of entrepreneurial education, as to which entrepreneurial education, as to which entrepreneurial characteristics can be developed to produce good entrepreneurs.

Vij & Sharma (2013) examined the entrepreneurial drive of business students and explored the effects of demographics on the entrepreneurial drive of students. An entrepreneurial drive scale developed by Florin et al., (2007) was used to measure the entrepreneurial drive of the students. The results showed that gender and family type do not significantly affect the entrepreneurial drive of business students. However, the mean score for the students (pre-entrepreneurial education and post-entrepreneurial education) was found to be significantly higher for two dimensions viz., self- efficacy and non-conformity out of the five dimensions of entrepreneurial drive. The study proved that entrepreneurial education enhances self-efficacy of the students and gives them confidence to be non-conformists. For three other dimensions of entrepreneurial drive-preference for innovation, achievement motivation and proactive disposition, there was hardly any change in the mean score values after entrepreneurial education.

Begam et.al., (2012) built on psychological model based on Ajzen's theory of planned behaviour to identify the factors influencing the entrepreneurial intention of these students. It is suggested that educational system which provides adequate knowledge and inspiration for entrepreneurship develop the students' intention to perform entrepreneurial behaviours and the possibility of choosing an entrepreneurial career might increase among young people. This study confirms the key role of educational support in the development of entrepreneurial intention. Therefore, the current study shows that entrepreneurship can be fostered through learning process.

Edwards (2012), conducted a study on the topic 'Evaluating Enterprise Education: Why Do It? The purpose of this paper was to argue that evaluations of enterprise education need to develop beyond the economist viewpoint of business start-up and business growth and promote the notion that evaluations of enterprise education should encompass prime pedagogical objectives of enterprise education, enabling students to grow and develop and to shape their own identities in the light of their learning experiences. The findings of the study reveals that the graduates who start their own businesses are reluctant to call themselves "entrepreneurs"; they question the meaning of the word and its relevance to them and findings suggest that "Entrepreneur" is a label given to them by educators and peers. The study has proven to be useful in improving the format, content and delivery of enterprise education on campus and also the development of appropriate evaluation tools.

Udoukpong, Emah & Umoren (2012) in their study aimed to explore the difference in junior secondary students 'academic performance in Entrepreneurial Curriculum of Business Studies based on their attitudes to the subject, parental influence, and career aspirations. The sample comprised of 290 students from 9th grade from eight (four urban and four rural) public secondary schools in Akwaibom State of Nigeria. Sample was obtained through stratified random sampling and proportional sampling techniques. Data was collected through Personal Characteristics Variables Questionnaire which composed of 10 Likert-scale items on each of the personal characteristic variable's attitudes, parental influence and career aspirations. Major findings revealed that students 'academic performance in Business Studies differed significantly on the basis of attitudes and parental influence, (ii) The variable of career aspirations made no significant difference in the students 'academic achievement in Business Studies. Further suggestions included implications for school and teachers 'consideration of students 'characteristics in implementation of Business Studies curriculum.

Korhonen's (2012) in the study on "Not Everyone Is Cut out to be the Entrepreneur Type": How finish school teachers construct the meaning of entrepreneurship education and the related abilities of the pupils set out to explore how a group of finish school teachers constructs the meaning of entrepreneurship education and produces related characterizations of the abilities of the pupils in their interviews. In their discussions, the teachers deployed the discourses of "internal entrepreneurship" and "external entrepreneurship". Internal entrepreneurship was associated with the pupils' responsible attitude to (school) work; it was represented as an ideal subjectivity for all and accepted as natural aim of schooling. The promotion of external entrepreneurship, however, was seen to be beyond the aims of basic education. Within the discourse of external entrepreneurship, the teachers explicated the differences between the pupils' abilities; they saw potential for entrepreneurship particularly in those boys who are not academically accomplished but are socially talented, creative, easy-going and risk-taking or competent at practical things. High performing students, especially girls, were not included in the characterizations of "the entrepreneurial type of pupil".

Rahmawati, Hasyyati & Yusran (2012) identify in their study six main groups of youth entrepreneurship barriers - named by them obstacles. Those six areas of obstacles are: insufficient knowledge and education, environment not enabling for youth entrepreneurship, economic and financial barriers, regulatory barriers, lack of relevant networks and lack of role models in entrepreneurship. Although study provided important information on barriers of youth entrepreneurship in Indonesia the classification of barriers itself seem not intuitive - for example by including fear of failure in category of education and knowledge or by creating separate category just for lack of role models.

Gondim & Mutti (2011) conducted a study on the topic "Affections in Learning Situations: A study of Entrepreneurship Skills Development Course". This study aims to present the results of a study whose general objective was to characterize the affective states experienced in response to different teaching activities used in workshop for developing entrepreneurship skills. It seeks to answer the following questions. How affections and experiential learning strategies interrelate in the development of entrepreneurial skills. The results suggest that the structure of the course favoured the predominance of affective states such as joy, excitement, pleasure, and pride. Activities similar to real situations generate greater emotional impact. It was also found that indirect learning activities and interactive activities are associated with lower levels of anxiety.

Jusoh, Ziyae, Asimiran & Kadir (2011) conducted a study on the topic "Entrepreneur Training Needs Analysis: Implications on the Entrepreneur Skills Needed for Successful Entrepreneurs". This study revealed the business competencies needed for successful in their business. The training needs for entrepreneurs identified and analysed with respect to a number of issues affecting business such as creativity and innovation, source of business finance, accounting skills, financial management are the areas in which the entrepreneurs find it difficult to acquire knowledge. The study confirms the view that entrepreneurship education makes a significant difference in the performance of entrepreneurs, with entrepreneurs expressing a need for further training and education in specific business issues.

Ali et. al., (2011) in their study entitled "Entrepreneurial Attitudes among Potential Entrepreneurs" had explored that the entrepreneurial attitudes among potential entrepreneurs in Pakistan. Multi-stage sampling maximized representation. Four hundred and eighty Masters of business administration students (potential entrepreneurs) from six public sector Pakistani universities returned completed questionnaires. Three factors emerged: entrepreneurial acceptability, entrepreneurial intentions and personal factors. Moreover, the perceptions of the potential 58 entrepreneurs on locus of control, self-efficacy, subjective norms and instrumental readiness were also analysed. The majority of students showed generally positive attitudes towards entrepreneurship at all six universities. Overall, there was a significant difference between negative and positive attitudes. There was also some impact of demographic variables, such as university, parental income and profession. Both genders exhibited similar attitudes at most of the sample institutions. The implications for practice and policy are discussed.

Mclaughlin (2010) in his study presented an empirical testing of the relationships between career intentions, self-efficacy and emotional intelligence in the entrepreneurial sector. The role of emotional intelligence as an antecedent to entrepreneurial intentions and behaviours was examined. The study of students from diverse educational backgrounds and enrolment in an entrepreneurship course found that individuals with high entrepreneurial self-efficacy were more likely to have intentions and the desire to establish a new business.

Rayen (2010) in his study states that the significant correlation exists between entrepreneurship and personality traits variables, namely decision-making ability, economic motivation, managerial ability, problem recognition and risk-taking willingness. Their correlation co-efficient are statistically significant at five per cent level and states that four key factors influence a person to start or manage the tiny enterprises namely, achievement and support factor, interest factor, traditional status factor and economic necessity factor.

Kumar (2010) examined that the development of tourism entrepreneurship and development warrants a thoughtful policy framework. Given the wearing degree and potential for Tourism Development offered by different regions and States, there cannot be uniform and stenotype tourism plans and programs for tourism development in the country. The fact reminds that tourism development program to be effective need to context and the region specific. The sooner it is done the better will be tourism entrepreneurship development and in turn economic development in the country.

Tamizharasi and Panchanathan (2010) studied 120 entrepreneurs both male and female to identify the level of entrepreneurial attitude of entrepreneurs in Cuddalore district of Tamilnadu. The findings of the study reveal that the male entrepreneurs have greater entrepreneurial attitude than the female entrepreneurs. They also found that the entrepreneurial attitude increases as the age increases.

Maalu (2010) in his study aims to determine the factors influencing students' personal goals in life relative to entrepreneurship and to establish the students' perception of their own entrepreneurial ability. After considering different factors, the results suggest that goals in entrepreneurial ability are influenced by factors such as maximum utilization of own skills and talents, full control of own future, achievement of what one values personally. Freedom to make own decisions, financial security, opportunity to learn new things, perform challenging work, etc.

George & Samuel (2010) published an article on the topic "Impact of Globalization a Boon or Bane". The study pointed topic the globalization on the one hand has to overthrow many conventional employment opportunities due to the impact of is the ability to modern techniques. Entrepreneurship development program has to play an important role for upgrading of the knowledge and skills of the younger generation. Entrepreneurship is the ability to discover an investment opportunity and to organise an enterprise undertaking the risks involved, there by contributing to real economic growth. Globalization has led to an entrepreneurial of production. The greatest myth that was associated with entrepreneurship development was that entrepreneurs are born and in no way, they can be developed.

Liyas (2010), published an article on the topic "Entrepreneurs-Generation and Entrepreneurial Success- An Empirical Study". This study reveals that the industrialization plays a significant role in employment generation and economic development. The leather industry has significantly contributed to the nation's development and in earning sufficient foreign exchange by exporting finished leather industry entrepreneurs determined in this study is expected to provide the factor entrepreneur who wants to invest in leather industry with relevant insights. This is desirable, it has been proved in this study that first generation entrepreneur's success rate is higher than second generation entrepreneurs. Though the government is not granting permission for starting fresh tanneries because of influence problem, the existing industries may be further developed.

Adeyemo (2009) in the study understanding and acquisition of entrepreneurial skills: A pedagogical re-orientation for class room teacher in science education illuminates the basic procedure, stages and essential indices for acquiring entrepreneurial skills in the globalised teaching enterprise by teachers and students. The results revealed pedagogical strategies like co-operative learning strategies, case study, reciprocal peer questioning, conference style learning was effective for promoting entrepreneurial skills in science education.

Zaidatol & Abdullah (2009) in their study exploring the entrepreneurial mind-set of students: implication for improvement of entrepreneurial learning at university explored the entrepreneurial mind-set of students after following entrepreneurial education. Several teaching techniques were utilized to infuse entrepreneurial skills among learners by setting a modified version of entrepreneurial directed approach. Results revealed that the entrepreneurial directed approach developed entrepreneurial skills and behaviour of the students.

Schwarz et.al., (2009) examined the key factors influencing students' intent to create a new venture. The paper aims to develop a model of entrepreneurial intent that incorporates both human and environmental factors. The findings of the study show that, with the exception of the attitude toward competitiveness, all other paths regarding general and specific attitudes are significant. Pertaining to the environment conditions, only significant effects of the university on students' interest in business founding were detected.

Mir & Nizamuddin (2008) studied to identify students' attitudes and intentions toward entrepreneurship and their future plans in connection with starting their own business. This paper tests Entrepreneurial Intention - which is adapted from the Theory of Planned Behaviour. The results show that the conventional programs do not have the intended effects; the effect on students' entrepreneurial skills is insignificant and the effect on the intention to become an entrepreneur is even more significantly negative.

Audet (2008) studied that educational institutions have tried to respond to the growing popularity of entrepreneurship by offering a variety of courses in entrepreneurship and small business management. The thrust of such courses varies according to the clienteles at which they are aimed. Generally speaking, they serve as an introduction to the entrepreneurial field, they provide the skills, knowledge and abilities required for starting a venture and finally, they attempt to awaken and stimulate the Entrepreneurial Skills of participants. The objective of the study was to measure the impact of (1) the students' perceptions of the desirability and feasibility of starting their own venture, (2) their learning in terms of either skills or knowledge, and (3) their level of awareness to entrepreneurship and the small business context. Results from this experiment prompted a follow-up study in which the initial experiment was partially replicated.

Ertuna & Gurel (2008) investigated the effect of entrepreneurial traits and education on the entrepreneurial intentions of university students. They measured entrepreneurial intentions as well as entrepreneurial traits like need for achievement, risk-taking propensity, innovativeness, tolerance of ambiguity and locus of control. The results indicated that there was a statistically significant relationship between entrepreneurial intentions with entrepreneurial traits. Students with higher scores for innovation, propensity to take risk and occupational achievement had a higher entrepreneurial intention.

Wilson, Kickul & Marlino (2007) in their study entitled "Gender Entrepreneurship Self-Efficiency and Entrepreneurial Career Intention: Implication for Entrepreneurship Education" proved that self-efficacy, advocates of career decision being perceived as individual innermost thoughts that determine whether they had the abilities perceived as important to task performance as well as belief that they would be able and effectively convert their skills into chosen outcome. They also found that higher entrepreneurial self-efficacy and higher entrepreneurial intention result in an individual's higher probability of being involved in entrepreneurial activity later in his or her life. It followed therefore that even if entrepreneurial intentions did not result into a person starting a business, it was still important to prepare future entrepreneurs and could help us distinguish between would-be-entrepreneurs and non-entrepreneurs.

Vaidya (2007) conducted a study on developing entrepreneurial like skills and found entrepreneurial values can be developed in a social setting rather than only seen as an economic activity. The study highlighted that the complex phenomenon of entrepreneurship can be brought down to elementary stage in an integrated manner through inspirational ways fostering enterprising spirit life skills to face challenges of life.

Nieman & Vuuren (2006) in their study enhancing female entrepreneurship by enabling access to skills stressed the development of particular skills namely technical skills, business management skills and personal entrepreneurial skills through intervention programme. The results revealed that experimental group gained entrepreneurial and business skills after the completion of programme which showed improvement of entrepreneurial skills and business skills of females.

Gurol & Atssam (2006) in their study entitled "Entrepreneurial characteristics among University Students: Some Insights for Entrepreneurship Education and Training in Turkey" stated that much more people would seek to benefit from advantages associated with work values such as independence, challenge and self-actualization by setting up their own firms. Entrepreneurs enjoyed self-reassuring joy while they run businesses. There was more flexibility in self-employment than in a salaried job. People who traded as entrepreneurs also enjoy a sense of pride in the business they own. They were their own bosses who benefit from the effort they indulge in business by gaining profit

Jesselyn & Mitchell (2006) aimed to assess the state of development of entrepreneurship education, determine the importance of entrepreneurship in the South African higher education institutions (HEIs), and offer recommendations for improving preparations for the developing field. Results indicate that the entrepreneurship education in South Africa is in its developmental stage, although it is perceived as important in elevating the profile of any institution and there is increasing commitment from the institutions in academic, research and outreach offerings in entrepreneurship.

Collins et.al., (2006) described an exploration in the use of synergistic learning methods in the delivery of an innovative pilot programme designed to teach entrepreneurship capacities. The programme took a tripartite approach involving nascent entrepreneurs, existing entrepreneurs and facilitators using an action research and action learning approach. The paper describes innovative and effective methods to teach entrepreneurship capacities that mirror the real world experience of existing and nascent entrepreneurs.

Bhandari (2006) in his study "Inclination for Entrepreneurship among Students in India" studied group of university students in India who intended to do upon completion of their college educations. The respondents started their own business and become entrepreneurs or work for someone else. A 62-item questionnaire was administered to the first-year students of the Faculty of Commerce and Management Studies at Jai Narain Vyas University, Jodhpur, India. Of the 186 questionnaires returned, 100 were used for this study. From the results of chi-square tests of the eighteen independent variables, only two were found to have significant relationship with the dependent variable to start your own business. According to the results of factor analysis, six variables to lead other people, to be own boss, to put innovative ideas into practice, determination, personal challenge of no business education were found to relate to the dependent variable. Finally, the logistic regression analysis showed that these six factors had a 92.35 per cent predictive value.

Gurol & Atsan (2006) in their study "Entrepreneurial Characteristics amongst University Students - Some Insights for Entrepreneurship Education and Training in Turkey" explored the entrepreneurship profile of Turkish university students and made an evaluation for their entrepreneurship orientation by comparing them with non-entrepreneurially inclined students. In this study, six attitudes, namely need for achievement, locus of control, risk taking propensity, tolerance for ambiguity, innovativeness and self- confidence were used to define the entrepreneurial profile of students. The study was conducted on a random sample of fourth year university students from two Turkish universities. The entrepreneurial attitudes of these students were subjected to a comparative analysis with other students who do not plan to start their own business and thus were not included in the group of potential entrepreneurs. The results of the t-tests showed that except for tolerance for ambiguity and self-confidence, all entrepreneurial attitudes were found to be higher in entrepreneurially inclined students as compared to entrepreneurially non-inclined students. These students were found to have higher risk-taking propensity, internal locus of control, higher need for achievement and higher innovativeness.

Chawala & Butare (2005) in their article "Developing Entrepreneurial Competencies amongst Rwandan Youth" stated that the development of entrepreneurship was essential both for solving the problems of unemployment, for industrial development and balanced regional development. Most of the developing countries had adopted a deliberate policy of developing and encouraging small entrepreneurs as a strategy for the overall development. Entrepreneurship development was a human resource development process which dealt with the human motivation, skills, competence, social and economic risks and investment of financial and physical resources of the individual and the State. It was crucial for industrial development and for alleviating the problem of unemployment which was attaining alarming proportions all over the world. Entrepreneurship was not restricted to any regions or community; rather entrepreneurial potential could be found and developed in any place without consideration of age, qualification, experience or socio-economic backgrounds. This paper was an attempt to show that Rwandan educated youth possessed the competencies to be a successful entrepreneur provided they get support from the environment and society.

Baum & Locke (2004) in their study, "The Relationship of Entrepreneurial Attitudes, Skill and Motivation to Subsequent Venture Growth" found that entrepreneurship as well as goal, social-cognitive and leadership theories has guided hypotheses regarding the relationship between entrepreneurial attitudes and skill such as passion, tenacity, and new resource skill and situational specific motivation like communicated vision, self-efficacy and goals to subsequent venture growth. Data from 229 entrepreneur-chief executive officers and 106 associates in a single industry were obtained in a 6-year longitudinal study. Structural equation modelling revealed a web of relationships that impact venture growth. Goals, self-efficacy and communicated vision had direct effects on venture growth which were mediated the effects of passion, tenacity and new resource skill on subsequent growth. Furthermore, communicated visions sand self-efficacy was related to goals and tenacity was related to new resource skill.

DISCUSSION AND CONCLUSION

From the review of related literature, the researcher found that, most of the earlier studies are conducted among the professional and technical students. In few of the studies, the sample targeted to specific groups like women entrepreneurs, emerging entrepreneurs from rural India and so on. From the review of related literature, it is clear that, there is lack of studies among the B.Com students. Since India having an enormous young population there is a need of entrepreneurship education among the B.Com students. There are 27.2% of the population of India constitutes youth in the age group of 15-29. From the review of related literature, it is obvious that, the present study titled "Analysis of Entrepreneurial Traits among B.Com students" is unique and different from earlier studies.

3

Methodology

INTRODUCTION

The success of the research depends on the stability of the method adopted and the training that the researcher receives. Webster's Collegiate Dictionary defines research as "studious inquiry or examination; esp. investigation or experimentation aimed at the discovery and interpretation of facts, revision of accepted theories or laws in the light of new facts, or practical application of such new or revised theories or laws". It is actually the voyage of discovery.

Best (2006) defines "Educational research as that activity which is directed towards development of science of behaviour in educational situation. The ultimate aim of such a science is to provide knowledge that will permit the educator to achieve his goal by the most effective method".

Methodology is the procedure adapted in a research study or investigation. It occupies a very prominent position in any kind of research process. The success of any research depends on methodology, which determines the validity of results.

Methodology is the description of procedures or technique adopted in a research study or investigation. Methodology occupies a very important place in any type of research. As the validity and reliability of the findings depends on the method adopted. To conduct the research, the researcher has to select the methods and tools which are apt to this study. The selection of a method and a specific design within that method appropriate in investigating a research problem and upon the kind of data that the problems entail. A pre-planned and well described method will provide scientific and feasible plan for attacking the solving problem under investigation. (Koul, 2003)

Research methodology is a way to systematically solve the research problem. It may be understood as a science of studying how research is done scientifically. It is necessary for the researcher to know not only the research methods or techniques but also the methodology. It is a collective term for the structured process of conducting research. The aim of methodology is to help us to understand in the broadest possible terms, not the product of scientific inventory but the process itself. It has an important position in any kind of research as the validity and reliability of the findings depends upon the methods adopted. It outlines the entire research plan and includes the description of the techniques or methods and tools the researcher has used for collecting, organizing and analysing the data.

Methodology or the procedure adopted in any research study occupies a vital role as the success of any investigation depends largely upon the suitability of the method, tools and technique used for the collection of data. The vehicle of research cannot perform its function without it. Since it is methodology which lays out the way in which formed research is to be carried out and outlines the detailed description of research variables and procedures. (Barr, 1960).

In the words of Mertens (2010), research methodology is a scientific inquiry that is to collect, analyse and use the data to understand, describe, predict, or control an educational phenomenon or to empower individual in such contexts.

Research has three-fold objectives; theoretical, factual and application. These objectives are achieved by employing different methods and techniques of research. A researcher requires insight and discrimination to choose from among various methods which are adequate and useful for the study. The decision about the method for a research work significant, since it lays out the ways in which the formal research is to be carried out. The selection of method for research work depends upon the nature of the problem selected and the kind of data necessary for its solution. A suitable method helps the researcher to explore the diverse stands of the study and adequately measure them so as to satisfy the requirement and thus it is the means to an end.

The validity and reliability of the research findings depends on the method adopted. Method selected should always be appropriate to the nature of the problem under investigation and the kind of data that the problem depends. The present study is entitled as "Analysis of Entrepreneurial traits among B. Com students".

This chapter deals with the procedural details of the study which includes the design adopted, the sample chosen, tools used, procedure adopted and the statistical techniques employed for the analysis of data and the details pertaining to the study. The goal of this chapter is to explore the tools and techniques employed in the investigation.

OBJECTIVES OF THE STUDY

The investigators conducted the present study based on the following objectives.

1. To analyse the level of entrepreneurial traits among B.Com students.
2. To analyse the Entrepreneurial traits among B.Com students with respect to its components.
3. To analyse the entrepreneurial traits among B.Com students on the basis of gender.
4. To analyse the entrepreneurial traits among B. Com students on the basis of type of institution.
5. To analyse the entrepreneurial traits among B.Com students on the basis of locality.

HYPOTHESIS OF THE STUDY

The investigatorss conducted the present study based on the following hypothesis.

1. The entrepreneurial traits among B. Com students are poor.
2. There is no significant difference in the mean values of the various components of Entrepreneurial traits among B. Com students.
3. There is no significant difference in the entrepreneurial traits among B. Com students on the basis of gender.
4. There is no significant difference in the entrepreneurial traits among B. Com students on the basis of type of institution.
5. There is no significant difference in the entrepreneurial traits among B. Com students on the basis of locality.

METHOD ADOPTED FOR THE STUDY

The nature of the problem determines the type of data requires and the methods to be adopted in a study. To satisfy the objectives set for the study, the investigators adopted Normative Survey method for the present study. The normative survey investigates the conditions or relationship that exist, practices that prevail, beliefs, and point of view attitudes that are developing. It tries to bring out the normal or typical conditions or practices at present. And it also helps to provide information useful to the solution of problem because it involves the collection of information from individuals by the use of structured tools.

Survey research is designed to deal more directly with the nature of people's thoughts, opinions and feelings. According to Agarwal (2008), survey is devoted to the gathering of information about prevailing situations and is not simply analysing and tabulating data but includes proper analysis, interpretation, comparison and identification of trends and relationships. Survey studies are conducted to collect detailed description of existing phenomena with the aim of employing data to justify current conditions and practices or to make more intelligent plans for improving them.

DESIGN OF THE STUDY

"A research design is the arrangement conditions for collection and analysis of data in a manner that aims to combine relevance to the research variable's purpose with economy in procedure" (Kothari, 1990). The research design is the conceptual structure with in which research is conducted; it constitutes the collection of data, measurement and analysis of the data.

The present study was conducted among a sample of 200 students from various Government and Aided B. Com college students, Kottayam and Idukki districts, Kerala state. Simple Random sampling method was used for the selection of sample. Survey method was chosen for the study. The tool was developed and standardized by the investigators and has collected the relevant data regarding the study. The scores were analyses using appropriate statistical techniques such as mean, standard deviation, etc. are calculated for the sample and various sub sample, t-test, etc. also used for testing hypothesis, t-test was used for testing the significance of difference between means of different groups bases on gender, locality, and type of institution.

POPULATION, SAMPLE AND SAMPLING PROCEDURE

A population generally refers to any collection of specified groups of human being or non-human entities such as objects educational insinuations time units, geographical area, salaries etc. "The larger group of subjects to whom researcher is wish to apply their result constitute the population, which is a group of individuals or objects having at least one characteristic that distinguishes them from other groups". (Hittleman and Simon, 1997).

Sampling is the process by which a relatively small number of individuals, objects or events is selected and analysed in order to find out something about the entire population from which it was selected. It helps to reduce expenditure, save time and energy, permit measurement of greater precisions and accuracy. The representative proportion of the population is called a sample. (Chandra and Sharma, 2004).

The present study analyses the entrepreneurial traits among B.Com students. Hence the population of the present study is B.Com students from various Government and aided colleges of Kerala state. Measuring the entire population is impracticable through no entirely impossible. So, the investigators had to draw a sample from the population concerned. Sample is a small proportion of a population that is selected for observation and analysis. By observing the characteristics of the sample, one can make certain interference about the characteristics of the population from which it is drawn. (Best and Kahn, 2005).

Simple random sampling technique was employed in the present study so as to obtain an adequate sample with randomness and representativeness. The Kottayam and Idukki is selected and samples were taken from four colleges coming under Rural and Urban area. Separate lists of colleges prepared. Among the sample colleges selected, two are located in urban and two are located in rural areas which were selected randomly giving due representation to each stratum.

The universe of the study includes all the B.Com colleges in the Kerala state. And population of this study is the B.Com students of Kottayam and Idukki district. The researcher selected 200 B. Com students from Government and aided colleges in Kottayam and Idukki district. The details of the sample selected is given at Table 3.1

Table 3.1: Distribution of sample

No.	Name of the college	District	Type of Institution	Locality	No. of students
1.	Government College, Kottayam	Kottayam	Government	Urban	50
2.	CMS College, Kottayam	Kottayam	Aided	Urban	50
3.	Government Arts and Science College, Pooppara	Idukki	Government	Rural	50
4.	Pavanatma College, Murickassery	Idukki	Aided	Rural	50
	Total				**200**

Table 3.2: Breakup of the sample with respect to Gender of the students

Gender	No. of students
Male	100
Female	100
Total	**200**

Table 3.3: Breakup of the sample of students with respect to Type of Institution

Type of school	No. of students
Government	100
Aided	100
Total	**200**

Table 3.4: Breakup of the sample of students with respect to Locale of the institution

Locale of the college	No. of Students
Urban	100
Rural	100
Total	200

DESCRIPTION OF TOOLS AND TECHNIQUES ADOPTED

A great variety of research tools are of many kinds and employs distinctive ways of describing and qualifying the data. Each tool is particularly appropriate for certain sources of data yielding information of the kind and that would be most effectively used. Some of these devices merely identify the presence or absence of certain aspects of situations. Others collect qualitative descriptions which may involve comparisons or contracts between elements present in the situation. Other devices yield quantitative measures in scale measures or in scores. The measurement of what is identified adds an important dimension to description; not only what but how much is revealed. Many of the tools of research have been designed to yield quantitative measures. Others yield description that may be refined by counts of frequency of appearance. This qualification of data is an essential part of research. While some judgement cannot be expressed in frequency counts percentages, or scores, most data are made more meaningful by qualification. In addition to frequency counts and percentage or fractional comparisons, data may be refined by numerical ratings, rank order placement, paired comparisons, social distance scales, equal appearing intervals, summated ratings and standardized score values.

Tools of research are the instruments that are used for the collection of data and the selection of suitable instruments is very of the tool depends upon the type of the problem and appropriate tools and techniques are used for the collection of information in various ways. The researcher prepared necessary suitable tool to collect the data, viz. Entrepreneurial Traits assessment scale developed and standardised by Thamarasseri & Madhusoodhanan (2022). The above said tool is appended at the end of the dissertation.

Personal Information Schedule

The investigators prepared data schedule to collect personal details of the participants. It helps the investigators to collect the information such as name, gender, locality of the educational institution.

Entrepreneurial Traits Assessment Scale

It was decided to prepare an entrepreneurial traits assessment scale for students. This was prepared on the basis of 12 dimensions, viz. conceptual aspect, technical aspect, human relation aspect, communication aspect, decision-making aspect, managerial aspect, time management aspect, stress management aspect, personality and individual aspect, pioneering aspect, unification and organization aspect, computer knowledge aspect. There are 5 statements under each 12 dimensions and a total of 60 statements were prepared with the help of research guide. The investigators searched different types of books and previous reviews related entrepreneurial traits.

Preparation of the Initial Draft

To assess student's entrepreneurial traits, first a draft form of assessment scale was prepared on the basis of 12 dimensions. Items under each dimension were prepared after referring the literatures related to it and on conclusion with the supervising teacher. An initial tool of 70 statements was prepared by the investigators. It included positive and negative statements. The initial draft of the tool was submitted to the supervisor for evaluation. The supervisor scrutinized all the items constructed by the investigators. Out of 70 items prepared, certain items were changed on the basis of clarity and specificity.

Preparation of the Second Draft

The investigators implemented the suggestions given by the supervisor in the second draft. Long statements were split into specific statements and the items were then arranged in a meaningful and logical manner. The distribution of items in the scale (draft) are presented in Table 3.5.

Pilot study: The draft of the scale was administered to 100 randomly selected B.Com students for piolet study. Clear instructions were given to them. They were asked to respond to each statement by choosing any one of the five options which is most appropriate according to them. After administration of the tool, scoring was made as follows.

Scoring Procedure: The collected responses were scored. The entrepreneurial traits assessment scale is a five-point scale that consist of positive and negative statements. Scoring was done by awarding 5, 4, 3, 2 and 1 mark to the responses "always", "often", "sometimes", "rarely" and "never" respectively.

Table 3.5: Distribution of items in the draft form of Entrepreneurial Traits assessment scale

Sl. No.	Components	No. of Items
1.	Conceptual Aspect	6
2.	Technical Aspect	6
3.	Human Relation Aspect	6
4.	Communication Aspect	6
5.	Decision – making Aspect	6
6.	Managerial Aspect	6
7.	Time management Aspect	5
8.	Stress management Aspect	6
9.	Personality & Individual Aspect	6
10.	Pioneering/Risk taking Aspect	6
11.	Unification & Organisation Aspect	6
12.	Computer Knowledge Aspect	5
	Total	**70**

Table 3.6: Scores for positive and negative statements in the Entrepreneurial traits assessment scale

Sl. No.	Level of agreement	Score for positive statement	Score for negative statement
1.	Always	5	1
2.	Often	4	2
3.	Sometimes	3	3
4.	Rarely	2	4
5.	Never	1	5

Standardization Procedure: Item analysis is the process of analysing the items to select most relevant items in the pool. The statistical analysis of correlation is made use for this. The aim of item analysis is to accept or to reject items.

Table 3.7: 't' values of the Initial Statements framed for Entrepreneurial traits assessment scale

Question No.	t value	Selected Questions
(1)	(2)	(3)
1.	2.72	Accepted
2.	4.92	Accepted
3.	5.95	Accepted
4.	1.02	Rejected
5.	2.78	Accepted
6.	3.56	Accepted
7.	2.15	Accepted
8.	4.09	Accepted
9.	2.01	Accepted
10.	0.95	Rejected
11.	5.29	Accepted
12.	4.76	Accepted
13.	2.48	Accepted
14.	4.30	Accepted
15.	1.37	Rejected
16.	4.49	Accepted
17.	2.13	Accepted
18.	3.48	Accepted
19.	4.50	Accepted
20.	2.22	Accepted
21.	3.82	Accepted
22.	3.89	Accepted
23.	4.91	Accepted
24.	0.83	Rejected
25.	1.98	Accepted
26.	5.15	Accepted
27.	5.08	Accepted
28.	2.32	Accepted
29.	0.78	Rejected
30.	5.21	Accepted
31.	2.27	Accepted
32.	1.46	Rejected

(Table Contd...)

(1)	(2)	(3)
33.	3.89	Accepted
34.	4.27	Accepted
35.	4.54	Accepted
36.	2.35	Accepted
37.	4.78	Accepted
38.	3.30	Accepted
39.	3.77	Accepted
40.	3.84	Accepted
41.	3.07	Accepted
42.	2.65	Accepted
43.	2.04	Accepted
44.	3.58	Accepted
45.	3.56	Accepted
46.	4.85	Accepted
47.	1.78	Rejected
48.	4.42	Accepted
49.	5.92	Accepted
50.	4.81	Accepted
51.	3.34	Accepted
52.	3.83	Accepted
53.	0.69	Rejected
54.	3.79	Accepted
55.	7.14	Accepted
56.	3.42	Accepted
57.	2.45	Accepted
58.	5.02	Accepted
59.	0.87	Rejected
60.	1.13	Rejected
61.	2.24	Accepted
62.	3.75	Accepted
63.	6.72	Accepted
64.	4.58	Accepted
65.	4.68	Accepted
66.	2.80	Accepted
67.	2.14	Accepted
68.	4.35	Accepted
69.	7.19	Accepted
70.	6.12	Accepted

The standardization of Entrepreneurial traits assessment scale was done by item analysing 't' test. The quantitative analysis was done by finding out the t-values.

For item analysis of Entrepreneurial Traits assessment scale, the response sheets of 100 students were arranged in the ascending order of their ranks i.e., as per total score obtained by each individual for all items. The highest 27% and the lowest 27% were selected as the criterion groups in items of which to evaluate the individual items.

Then the numerical values of their mean response to each item. The 't' value for each statement is calculated by using the formula:

$$t = (x_1 - x_2)/\surd\ [(s_1/n_1) + (s_2/n_2)]$$

were,

x_1 = Observed Mean of 1st Sample

x_2 = Observed Mean of 2nd Sample

s_1 = Standard Deviation of 1st Sample

s_2= Standard Deviation of 2nd Sample

n_1 = Size of 1st Sample

n_2 = Size of 2nd Sample

Entrepreneurial Traits Assessment Scale (Final)

After conducting the try out, the investigators discarded 10 items in Entrepreneurial Traits assessment scale and prepared the final draft. The demographic part is included to collect information like Name, Gender, Type of Institution, Locality of the Institution, also contained an instructional part in order to make the scoring easier for the respondents. The respondents had to make (✓) in the given space according to his or her opinion. The items selected for the study is shown in the table 3.8.

Validity of the Test

"Validity refers to the degree to which evidence and theory support the interpretations of test scores entailed by proposed uses of tests" (Joint Committee on Standards for Educational and Psychological Testing, 1999). The validity of a test refers to how well the measure actually represents the true construct of interest- the thing we are trying to measure. It shows the degree of accuracy of the test when compared with the accepted criteria. The investigators ensured the face validity and content validity of the test by careful reference of the literature and with the consultation with experts. Thus, the validity of the scale was assessed and the scale was found to be reasonably valid for the present purpose.

Table 3.8: Details of the components and number of statements of Entrepreneurial traits assessment scale

No.	Components	Statement number	No. of items
1.	Conceptual Aspect	1, 2, 3, 4, 5	5
2.	Technical Aspect	6, 7, 8, 9, 10	5
3.	Human Relation Aspect	11, 12, 13, 14, 15	5
4.	Communication Aspect	16, 17, 18, 19, 20	5
5.	Decision making Aspect	21, 22, 23, 24, 25	5
6.	Managerial Aspect	26, 27, 28, 29, 30	5
7.	Time management Aspect	31, 32, 33, 34, 35	5
8.	Stress management Aspect	36, 37, 38, 39, 40	5
9.	Personality & Individual Aspect	41, 42, 43, 44, 45	5
10.	Pioneering/Risk taking Aspect	46, 47, 48, 49, 50	5
11.	Unification & Organization Aspect	51, 52, 53, 54, 55	5
12.	Computer Knowledge Aspect	56, 57, 58, 59, 60	5
	Total		**60**

Reliability of the Test

Reliability is the consistency with which a test measure what it does measure. The concept of reliability underlines the computation of the range of the 'error of measurement' of a single score, where by predict the range of fluctuation likely to occur in a single individual's score as a result of irrelevant chance factors.

There are four methods in common use for measuring the reliability of a test. They are:

1. Test – retest method
2. Alternate or parallel method
3. Split – half method
4. Method of rational equivalence

In the present study the investigators used Karl Pearson correlation coefficient under test-retest method.

$$r = \frac{N\,\Sigma xy - \Sigma x \varepsilon y}{\sqrt{(N\Sigma x^2 - (\Sigma x)^2(N\Sigma y^2 - (\Sigma y)^{2)}}}$$

r = Coefficient of correlation

N = Number of Students

Σx = Sum of score of the first half items

Σy = Sum of scores of the second half items

Collection of Data

Details regarding the sample, procedure employed for collection of data and consolidation of the collected data are described under this section.

Procedure for Data Collection

The investigators visited the selected colleges and obtained permission from the concerned authority of the college. The investigators could arouse real enthusiasm among the students and create a favourable and co-operative atmosphere by explaining the purpose, function and nature of the study. A brief instruction given so as to motivate the students to answer the tool honestly. A sincere effort was made to establish rapport with the students.The investigators gave specific instruction about filling up of personal profile. The investigators also demonstrated an example as to how the students should mark their responses on Entrepreneurial traits assessment scale. The place for response was given to the right side of each item. The investigators asked to put tick mark on appropriate column. The response sheets were collected from the students within an hour.

Scoring and Consolidation of Data

Scoring of the response sheets is done as per the scoring scheme of the scale. The data related to the sample under study were consolidated appropriately. The responses identified by the students were analysed and interpreted numerically.

STATISTICAL TECHNIQUES USED FOR THE STUDY

Statistical techniques provide an indispensable tool for collecting, analysing, and interpreting data. These methods can facilitate the derivation of conclusion and formulation of generalisations.The investigators for analysing the data used the following major statistical techniques.

(a) Arithmetic mean

(b) Median

(c) Mode

(d) Standard deviation

(e) Skewness

(f) Kurtosis

(g) t test

(h) ANOVA

Arithmetic Mean: Mean is the simplest measurement of central tendency and is a widely use measure. Mean is calculated using the following formula:

$$M = \frac{\sum fx}{N}$$

Were,

M = Arithmetic Mean

F = Frequency of the class interval

X = Mid value

N = Total number of students

Median: Median is the middle most score of a distribution i.e., it is the half way value of a distribution:

Median is calculated using the formula

$$\text{Median} = 1 + [N_2 - \tfrac{m}{f}]c$$

Were,

l = lower limit of median class

N = Total number of scores

m = sum of scores of all intervals

f = cumulative frequency up to the median class

c = class interval

Mode: Mode is the value of items, which occurs more frequently than all other items.

$$\text{Mode} = 3 \text{ median} - 2 \text{ mean}$$

Or

$$\text{Mode} = 1 + \frac{Cf_2}{f_1 + f_2}$$

1 = lower limit of the median class

c = width of the class interval

f_1 = frequency of the class just below the model class

f_2 = frequency of the class just above the model class

Standard deviation: Standard deviation is the measure of dispersion of a set of data from its mean. It measures the absolute variability of a distribution; the higher the dispersion or variability, the greater is the standard deviation and greater will be the magnitude of the deviation of the value from their mean. The standard deviation is the most stable index of variability and is the customarily employed in experimental work and in research studies. In the present study the investigators computed the standard deviation using the formula.

$$SD = c\sqrt{\frac{\Sigma fd^2}{N} - \left(\frac{\Sigma fd}{N}\right)^2}$$

Were,

f = frequency of each class

d = deviation of each score from the assumed mean

N = total sample

C = class interval

Skewness: The word skewness means 'lack of symmetry'. In a normal distribution mean, median and mode coincide. Then the right and left half in the curve will be in symmetry. The distance between the mean and the median will indicate the extent of skewness.The degree of skewness in a frequency distribution may be calculated with the help of the formula.

$$Sk = \frac{3\ (mean\ -\ median)}{\sigma}$$

$$\sigma = SD$$

Kurtosis: Kurtosis is often described as the extent to which the peak of a probability distribution deviates from the shape of a normal distribution (if it is more pointed the distribution is leptokurtic, if it is flatter, it is platykurtic). Since 'outlying values' are the most influential, a more useful way to regard kurtosis is in terms of tail length (if the tails are longer than expected it is platykurtic, if shorter it is leptokurtic).

$$Ku = \frac{Q}{P_{90} - P_{10}}$$

Were,

Q = quartile deviation

$P_{90} = 1 + \left(\frac{90N}{100} - \frac{N}{f}\right)C$

$P_{10} = 1 + \left(\frac{10N}{100} - \frac{M}{f}\right)C$

t-test: t-test is a statistical that is used to compare the means of two groups. It is often used in hypothesis testing to determine whether a process or treatment actually has an effect on the population of interest, or whether two groups are different from one another. In this study investigators used t-test for the samples and it is helpful to check the significance difference in the mean scores.

$t = (x_1 - x_2)/\sqrt{}\ [(s_1/n_1) + (s_2/n_2)]$

x_1 = Observed Mean of 1st Sample

x_2 = Observed Mean of 2nd Sample

s_1 = Standard Deviation of 1st Sample

s_2 = Standard Deviation of 2nd Sample

n_1 = Size of 1st Sample

n_2 = Size of 2nd Sample

One way ANOVA: The value of ANOVA in testing experimental hypothesis is most strikingly demonstrated in those case in which the significance of the difference among more than two means is desired. In ANOVA, the F value indicates whether there exists significant difference between means. Calculation of one-way ANOVA is given below.

Step 1

Correction term $C_x = \frac{\Sigma x^2}{N}$

Step 2

Total sum of squares (ss) for X = $\Sigma x^2 - C_x$

Step 3

Sum of squares among mean, X= $\frac{(\Sigma x_1)^2 + ({}^{2}_{\Sigma x_2}) - Cx}{N}$

Step 4

Sum of squares within groups

X = Total SS for X – Among group mean SS for X

Step 5

$$F = \frac{\textit{Mean squares of among the group}}{\textit{Mean squares within the group}}$$

Conclusion

Research methodology refers to the ways or methods that are used by a researcher to conduct research to attain the objectives. The research methodology part is quite important due to its quality and helps in identifying the ways of research that is conducted to solve a research issue. Additionally, to explore the research problem in effective and efficient manner, research methodology plays a fundamental role that also indicates the importance of this part of research. Here, the investigators used the most appropriate and suitable method for conducting the study, being within the limitation. It helped the investigators to explore the diverse stands of the study and adequately measure the scores, so as to satisfy the requirements.

Analysis and Interpretation of Data

INTRODUCTION

A systematic organization, classification and tabulation of data are the bench marks of a good research study. Goode and Hatt (1952) points out that analysis is amongst the first of the methods which a researcher will call upon his effort to reduce a field of size, that is, to extract a manageable chunk from the infinite complexity of real world.

Since the vast amount of data obtained from the administration of numerous instruments to the chosen sample is unprocessed, it must be analysed and evaluated in order to reach reliable conclusions and make accurate generalisations. In order to determine the underlying truths and meanings of the complicated tabulated data, it is necessary to break it down into simpler pieces and reassemble it in novel ways. It is a higher order intellectual ability that separates information into its component components to investigate understanding by classification, comparison, illustration, investigation, and other closely connected tasks carried out to find solutions to research aims (Gerard, 2010). "Analysis and Interpretation is the heart of the research report. Statistical analysis is the mathematical process of gathering, organizing, analysing and interpreting numerical data and is of the basic phases of the research process" (Best and Kahn, 2014). Analysing data involves looking at the ordered information to find underlying truths. To uncover the novel facts, the data are examined from as many perspectives as is practical. The results of the analysis must be carefully, logically, and critically examined in order to be properly interpreted. This inspection must take into account the limitations of the sample chosen and the instrument chosen and employed in the study. (Koul, 2007).

Analysis of data means studying the tabulated material in order to determine inherent facts or meanings. (Anastasi, 1968). The purpose of the analysis is to reduce data to intelligible and interpretable forms so that the relations of research problems can be studied and tested (Best & Kahn, 2010). The data may be adequate, valid, and reliable to extent, it does not serve any worthwhile purpose unless it is carefully edited, symmetrically classifies, tabulated, scientifically analysed, intelligently interpreted, and rationally concluded (Sindhu, 1997).

Analysis is a detailed and thorough procedure designed to investigate the underlying connections between distinct data. It is an important step in any research programme because it is the findings from this process that allow the researcher to draw the appropriate conclusions. After analysis, the results must be carefully, logically, and critically examined while bearing in mind the limitations of the sample chosen and the tool chosen and employed in the study. Essentially, the interpretation process consists of stating what the results indicate (Koul, 1984). editing includes evaluating the information gathered for accuracy, usefulness, and completeness. Classifying is the precise mathematical split of information into the content that is classed. The degree of significance was primarily used to interpret the study's findings. The validity of the relevant hypothesis was assessed toward the end of the interpretation, as stated by Garrett (1981)

The study's significance and consequences are made obvious through interpretation. Without interpretation, analysis cannot be finished, and without interpretation, interpretation cannot move further. Finding a connection or the study's place within the larger analytical framework is the responsibility of the interpretations. It ties the results to accepted theories or the body of information that is already available in a given field of study. The submitted hypotheses will be accepted or rejected based on a critical analysis of the findings, which will advance knowledge in the relevant field.

Hypothesis formulated for the study are stated below:

- The entrepreneurial traits among B.Com students are poor.
- There is no significant difference in the mean values of the various components of Entrepreneurial traits among B.Com students.
- There is no significant difference in the entrepreneurial traits among B.Com students on the basis of gender.
- There is no significant difference in the entrepreneurial traits among B.Com students on the basis of type of institution.
- There is no significant difference in the entrepreneurial traits among B.Com students on the basis of locality.

The collected data were consolidated, analysed, and interpreted for the realisation of the objectives of the study which are restated below:

- To analyse the level of entrepreneurial traits among B.Com students.
- To analyse the Entrepreneurial traits among B.Com students with respect to its components.
- To analyse the entrepreneurial traits among B.Com students on the basis of gender.
- To analyse the entrepreneurial traits among B.Com students on the basis of type of institution.
- To analyse the entrepreneurial traits among B.Com students on the basis of locality.

The data of the present study was analysed using appropriate statistical techniques as per the objectives of the study. The analysis and interpretation are presented below under the following major sections. The analysis and interpretation of the data collected through the study is given below:

ENTREPRENEURIAL TRAITS AMONG B.COM STUDENTS

The scores obtained from the Entrepreneurial Traits Assessment scale were collected and calculated the measures of central tendency, dispersion, skewness, and kurtosis. The details are given in table 4.1.

Table 4.1: Descriptive statistics for score regarding Measures of central tendency, measures of dispersion, skewness, and kurtosis of scores on Entrepreneurial traits for total sample

Entrepreneurial Traits	N	Mean	Median	SD	Sk	Ku
	200	223	224	24.0	-0.299	0.298

The Table 4.1 shows that the arithmetic mean for the total sample is 224 and standard deviation is 24. The maximum possible score that can be obtained from entrepreneurial traits assessment scale is 300 and the least is 60. This shows that the Entrepreneurial Traits among B.Com students are found at average level. The distribution is negatively skewed since the value of skewness is -0.299. This means the number of students who got high scores was comparatively higher than those who got low scores in the group, in indicates that scores are massed at the high end. Kurtosis of the scores is 0.298 which, is greater than the normal value 0.263. Therefore, the distribution is leptokurtic.

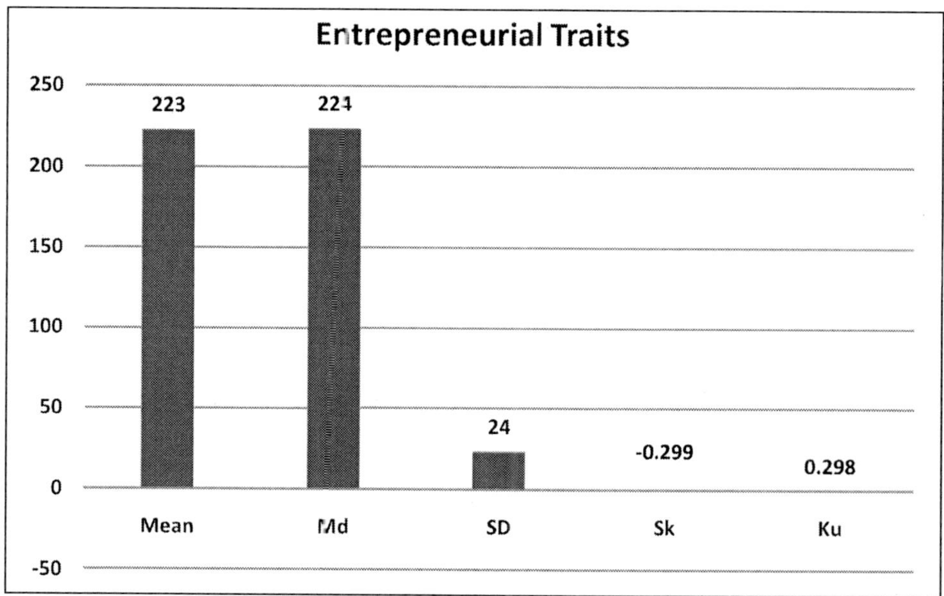

Figure 4.1: Descriptive statistics for score regarding Measures of central tendency, measures of dispersion, skewness, and kurtosis of scores on Entrepreneurial traits for total sample

Level of Entrepreneurial Traits Among B.Com Students for the Total Sample

The present chapter comprises of objective wise analysis of the data collected from B.Com students in Kerala. With regards to the objective, the present section of this chapter analyses the level of entrepreneurial traits among B.Com students according to objectives of the study in order to have a clear understanding of the results.The objective of the study is to know the extent of Entrepreneurial Traits among B.Com students. For this, investigators find out the mean and SD of the data obtained by administering the Entrepreneurial Traits assessment scale. Here three levels are considered namely high, average and low. This gives a picture about how much percentage of the sample comes in the high group, how much percentage in the average group and how much percentage in the low group.

For identifying the level of entrepreneurial traits among B.Com students, the students were classified into the High, Average and Low groups based on their scores obtained from the Entrepreneurial Traits assessment scale. Assuming a normal distribution of Entrepreneurial Traits assessment scores, the conventional procedure of using sigma distances was used for classifying sample. Considering the baseline of the normal curve representing the distribution extending from -3σ to +3σ, i.e., over a range of; B.Com students whose Entrepreneurial Traits assessment scores fall between M+ σ and M- σ were classified as 'Average – Entrepreneurial

Group'. B.Com students whose scores were below M- σ were classified as 'Low Entrepreneurial Traits Group' and B.Com students whose scores were above M+ σ were classified as 'High – Entrepreneurial Traits Group'.

For the distribution of Entrepreneurial Traits Assessment scores, mean was 223 and standard deviation was 24. Therefore, B.Com students whose Entrepreneurial Traits assessment scores were 247 or more were considered to possess 'Entrepreneurial Traits', whose scores less than 199 were considered to possess 'Low – Entrepreneurial Traits', and the remaining who come in between these scores were classified as of 'Average-Entrepreneurial Traits'. The data and the results of the classification done are shown in the Table 4.2.

Table 4.2: The classification of B.Com students in each of the groups based on the scores of Entrepreneurial traits assessment scale

	Group	Norms	Scores	N	Percentages
Entrepreneurial Traits	Low	M- σ	138	31	15.5%
	Average	M- σ to M+ σ	199 to 247	131	65.5%
	High	M+ σ	247	38	19%

To test the significance difference between the mean values of Entrepreneurial Traits Assessment scores of high, average, and low entrepreneurial traits among B.Com students, ANOVA is used. Details are given in the table 4.3

Table 4.3: Summary of ANOVA

	Group	N	Mean	SD	F	p
Entrepreneurial Traits	Low	31	186	14.15	284	.001
	Average	131	222	12.58		
	High	38	256	8.75		

The calculated 'F' value is 281. The table value of F for degrees of freedom (2,197) is 5.30 at 0.05 level and 4.61 at 0.01 level. From this it is clear that the computed F – value is greater than the table value (F = 284 with df (2, 197); $p<0.01$. It indicates that there is a significant difference between the mean values of Entrepreneurial Traits Assessment scores based on high, average, and low entrepreneurial traits among B.Com students.

ENTREPRENEURIAL TRAITS AMONG B.COM STUDENTS BASED ON ITS COMPONENTS

In this section the scores of each component from the Entrepreneurial Traits Assessment scale were separately found out and calculated Arithmetic mean. The details are given in the table 4.4.

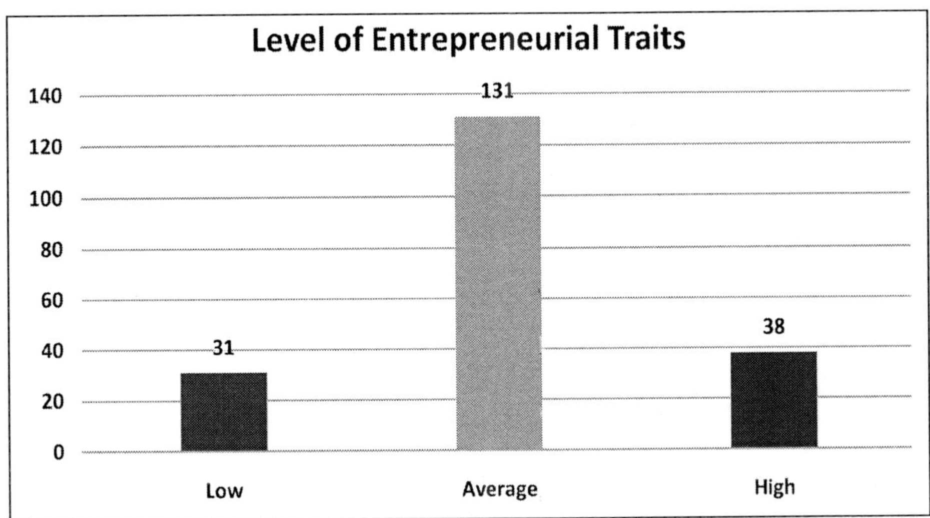

Figure 4.2: The classification of B.Com students in each of the groups based on the scores on Entrepreneurial Traits Assessment scale

Table 4.4: Mean values of components regarding Entrepreneurial traits

No.	Components	Mean Values
1.	Conceptual Aspect	18.135
2.	Technical Aspect	18.605
3.	Human Relation Aspect	21.155
4.	Communication Aspect	18.545
5.	Decision – Making Aspect	17.75
6.	Managerial Aspect	20.19
7.	Time Management Aspect	18.07
8.	Stress Management Aspect	17.395
9.	Personality & Individual Aspect	18.14
10.	Pioneering Skill/ Risk taking Aspect	19.115
11.	Unification & Organization Aspect	17.7
12.	Computer Knowledge Aspect	18.485

From the table 4.4, it is clear that the mean values of each component are different. Human Relation Aspect is higher when compared to other Entrepreneurial Traits components. Human relations in the institutional administration are the kind of relations that exist between the principal, administrators, teachers, workers and students among themselves, dictated by their religion and the interest of their nation, creating an atmosphere of trust and mutual respect and cooperation among them, especially the institutional manager to understand the feelings of students and sensitize their problems and work on solve them and achieve stability and meet the needs and thus derive satisfaction.

The mean value 17.39 of stress management aspect implies that B.Com students are poor in stress management when compared to other components. This may reduce the entrepreneurial traits among B.Com students. Therefore, the institutional administrators should give due care in organising certain stress management activities. From the table, it is evident that there exists a significant difference in the mean scores of various components of entrepreneurial traits among B.Com students.

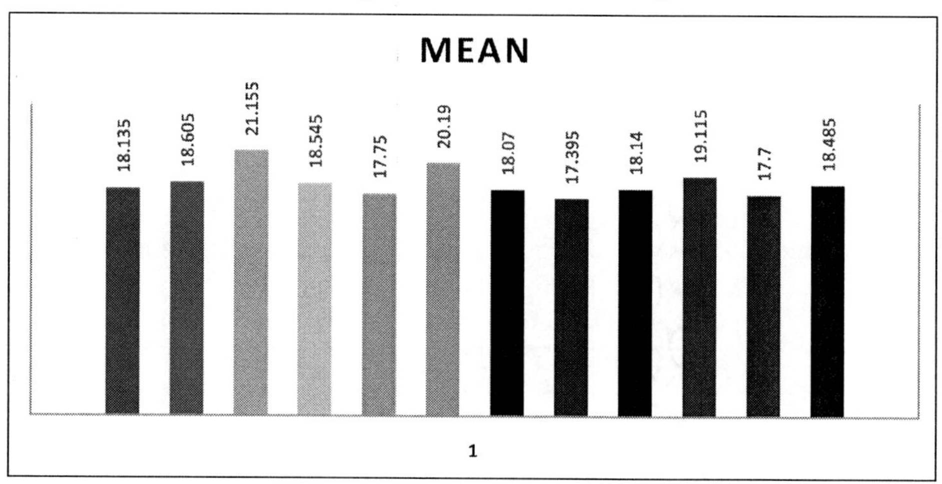

Figure 4.3: Mean values of components regarding Entrepreneurial Traits

ENTREPRENEURIAL TRAITS AMONG B.COM STUDENTS ON THE BASIS OF GENDER

In this section the Entrepreneurial Traits Assessment scores of males and female were separately found out and calculated Arithmetic mean, median Standard deviation, Skewness and Kurtosis. The details are given in the table 4.5.

Table 4.5: Measures of Central tendency, measures of dispersion, skewness, and kurtosis of Scores on Entrepreneurial traits based on Gender

Gender	N	Mean	Median	SD	Skewness	Kurtosis
Male	100	224	222	23.9	-0.0457	-0.619
Female	100	222	224	24.2	-0.545	1.17

The Table 4.5 shows the arithmetic mean for male is 224 and that for female is 222 and standard deviations are 23.9 and 24.2 respectively. This shows that the Entrepreneurial Traits among Female is lower than that of male. The value of median obtained for male group is 222 and that for female is 224 which shows that 50 percent of the male students have scored above 222 and 50 percent of female group scored above 224. Both the distribution is negatively skewed since the values of the skewness are - 0.0457 and – 0.545. This means the number of students who got high score was comparatively higher than those who got the low scores in the group. It indicates that scores are massed at the high end. Kurtosis of the scores is – 0.619 for male group which is less than the normal value 0.263 and for the girls is 1.17 which is greater than the normal value 0.263. Therefore, the distribution is platykurtic for male and leptokurtic for female.

Comparison of Entrepreneurial Traits among B.Com students based on Gender

For this the scores of boys and girls that was obtained from the Entrepreneurial Traits assessment scale were separated and computed their mean and standard deviation and thus found the significance of difference between the mean values by calculating the t value

Table 4.6: Data and the result of Test of significance of difference between mean values of Entrepreneurial Traits assessment scores based on Gender

Gender	N	Mean	SD	t
Male	100	224	23.9	0.49
Female	100	222	24.2	

The arithmetic mean and standard deviation of male group is 224 and 23.9 and that for female is 222 and 24.2. The t value obtained is 0.49 which is less than the table value 1.96 at 0.05 level. This indicate that there is no significant difference in mean scores of Entrepreneurial Traits among male and female students.

ENTREPRENEURIAL TRAITS AMONG B.COM STUDENTS ON THE BASIS OF TYPE OF INSTITUTION

In this section the Entrepreneurial traits assessment scores of Governments and Aided students were separately found out and calculated arithmetic mean, median, standard deviation, skewness and kurtosis. The details are given in the table 4.7.

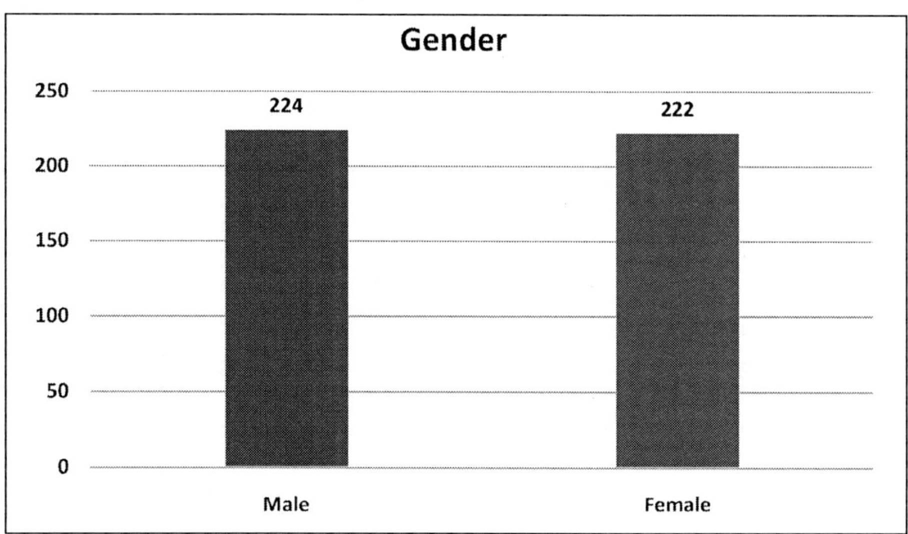

Figure 4.4: Bar diagram showing comparison of Entrepreneurial Traits among B.Com students based on Gender

Table 4.7: Measures of central tendency, measures of dispersion, skewness, and kurtosis of score on Entrepreneurial Traits Assessment based on Type of Institution

Type of Institution	N	Mean	Median	SD	Skewness	Kurtosis
Government	100	224	223	23.9	-0.0823	-0.0845
Aided	100	222	226	24.2	-0.428	0.463

This Table 4.7 shows the arithmetic mean for Government students is 224 and 222 for Aided college students and standard deviations are 23.9 and 24.2 respectively. This shows that the Entrepreneurial traits among Government students is higher than that of Aided college students. The value of median obtained for Government students is 223 and that of aided students is 222. From the median it is evident that 50 percent of Government college students have scored above 223 and 50 percent of Aided college students have scored above 226. Both the distributions are negatively skewed since the value of skewness are -0.0823 and -0.428. This means the number of students who got high score was comparatively higher than those who got the low scores in the group. It indicates that scores are massed at the high end. Kurtosis of the scores is -0.0845 for Government students' group which is less than the normal value 0.263 and for the Aided student's group is 0.463which is greater than the normal value 0.263. Therefore, the distribution is platykurtic for Government group and leptokurtic for Aided Group.

Comparison of Entrepreneurial Traits among B.Com students based on Type of Institution

For this the scores of Government group and Aided group that was obtained from the Entrepreneurial Traits assessment scale were separated and computed their mean and standard deviation and thus found the significance of difference between the mean values by calculating the t value.

Table 4.8: Data and the result of Test of significance of difference between mean values of Entrepreneurial Traits assessment scores based on Type of Institution

Gender	N	Mean	SD	t
Government	100	224	22.49	0.50
Aided	100	222	25.43	

The arithmetic mean and standard deviation of Government group is 224 and 22.49 and that for Aided group is 222 and 25.43. The t value obtained is 0.50 which is less than the table value 1.96 at 0.05 level. This indicate that there is no significant difference in mean scores of Entrepreneurial Traits among Government and Aided students.

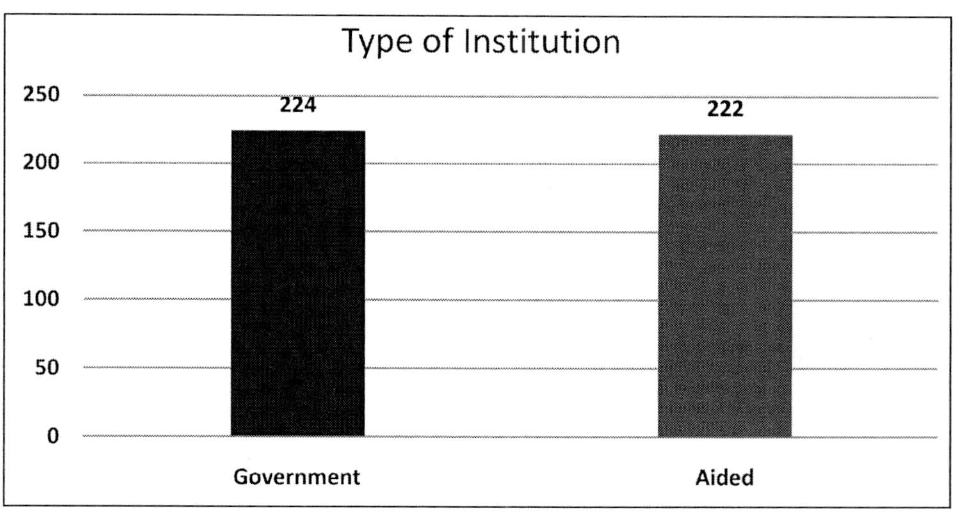

Figure 4.5: Bar diagram showing comparison of Entrepreneurial Traits among B.Com students based on Type of Institution

ENTREPRENEURIAL TRAITS AMONG B.COM STUDENTS ON THE BASIS OF LOCALITY

In this section the Entrepreneurial traits assessment scores of students who studying in Urban and Rural areas were separately found out and calculated arithmetic mean, median, standard deviation, skewness and kurtosis. The details are given in the table 4.9

Table 4.9: Measures of central tendency, measures of dispersion, skewness, and kurtosis of score on Entrepreneurial Traits Assessment based on Locality

Locality	N	Mean	Median	SD	Skewness	Kurtosis
Rural	100	224	224	22.4	0.0844	0.183
Urban	100	222	223	25.5	-0.533	0.243

This Table 4.9 shows the arithmetic mean for Rural group is 224 and 222 for Urban group students and standard deviations are 22.4 and 25.5 respectively. This shows that the Entrepreneurial traits among Rural group students is higher than that of Urban group students. The value of median obtained for Rural group is 224 and that of urban group is 223. From the median it is evident that 50 percent of students who studying in rural area have scored above 224 and 50 percent of students who were studying in urban area have scored above 223. The distribution for rural group students is positively skewed, which means the number of students who got high scores was comparatively lower than those who got the low scores in rural group. And the distribution for urban group students is negatively skewed, which means the number of students who got high scores was comparatively higher than those who got low scores in Urban group. It indicates that scores of Rural groups are massed at the low end and scores of Urban groups is marked at the high end. Kurtosis of the scores is 0.183 for Rural group and 0.243 for urban group which is less than the normal value 0.263. Therefore, the distribution is platykurtic.

Comparison of Entrepreneurial Traits among B.Com students based on Locality

For this the scores of Rural group and Urban group that was obtained from the Entrepreneurial Traits assessment scale were separated and computed their mean and standard deviation and thus found the significance of difference between the mean values by calculating the t value.

Table 4.10: Data and the result of Test of significance of difference between mean values of Entrepreneurial Traits assessment scores based on Locality

Locality	N	Mean	SD	t
Rural	100	224	22.42	0.60
Urban	100	222	25.49	

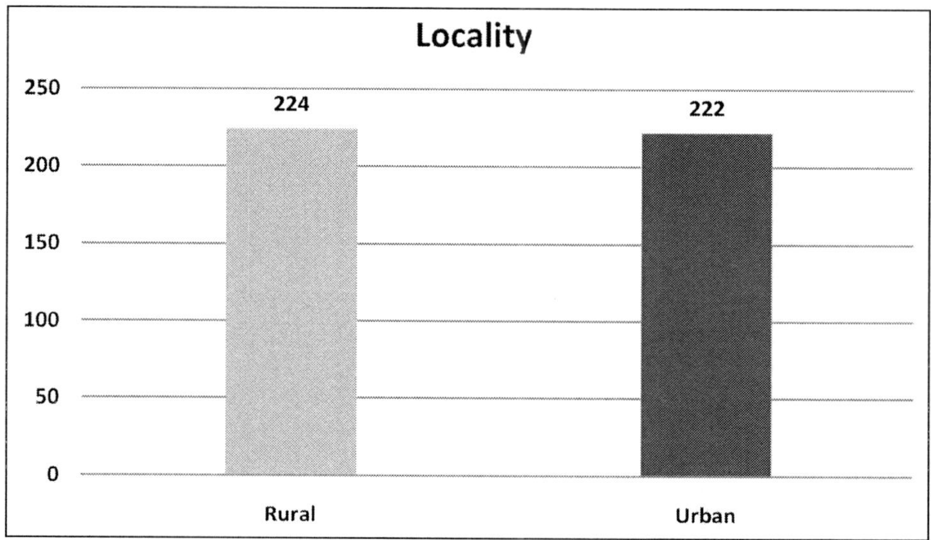

Figure 4.6: Bar diagram showing comparison of Entrepreneurial Traits among B.Com students based on Locality of Institution

The arithmetic mean and standard deviation of Rural group is 224 and 22.42 and that for Urban is 222 and 25.49. The t value obtained is 0.60 which is less than the table value 1.96 at 0.05 level. This indicate that there is no significant difference in mean scores of Entrepreneurial Traits among Rural and Urban students.

Findings, Suggestions and Conclusion

INTRODUCTION

Every research procedure strives to conduct a methodical and impartial analysis of the data gathered. This aids the researcher in drawing reliable findings from data analysis using statistics. The analysis's results are explained in light of the circumstances of the experiment. On the basis of these reliable results, sound generalisations are established. This prompts a discussion on the study's educational implications in the current environment and results in recommendations for performing additional research in the relevant field. The process's final stage, summarising the study, calls for critical and logical thinking.

STUDY IN RETROSPECT

On the back of the findings and discussion; the concluding chapter of this dissertation attempts to derive the educational implications of the present study. In addition, this chapter will also include recommendations for the teachers, school administrators, state, policy makers and parents with regard to entrepreneurial traits. This chapter will wrap up with suggestions for further research and conclusion.The present study was intended to find out the "Entrepreneurial Traits Among B.Com Students".This chapter intends to prove an overview of the significant aspects of the stages in conducting the study and the important findings and suggestions for the further study.

METHODOLOGY IN BRIEF

In the present study, normative survey method was employed by the investigators. Simple random sampling technique was used in this study.

By giving sufficient weightage to the factors like gender, type of institution, locality of the institution, a sample of 200 B.Com students from two districts of Kerala were selected for the study.

CONCLUSION BASED ON FINDINGS OF THE STUDY

Conclusion 1: Most of the B.Com students possess an average level (65.5%) of Entrepreneurial Traits. Objective 1 set for the study "To analyse the level of Entrepreneurial Traits among B.Com students" was based on the hypothesis 1 which states that "The level of Entrepreneurial traits among B.Com students is low". The conclusion 1 for the above objective is arrived based on the statistical analysis and is supported by the following findings.

Findings 1.1: There are 65.5 % of B.Com students possess an average level of Entrepreneurial traits. Whereas, 19% of B.Com students have high level of Entrepreneurial traits, and 15.5 % of them having Entrepreneurial traits at a low level.

Conclusion 2: There exists significant difference in the mean values of the various components of Entrepreneurial traits among B.Com students. Objective 2 set for the study "To analyse the Entrepreneurial traits among B.Com students with respect to its components" was based on the hypothesis 2 which state that "There is no significant difference in the mean values of the various components of Entrepreneurial traits among B.Com students. The conclusion 2 for the above objective is arrived based on the following findings.

Findings 2.1: The mean scores of various components of entrepreneurial traits are different. The component which has highest mean score is Human relation aspect (21.155) and the lowest is Stress Management Aspect (17.395).

Conclusion 3: There exists no significant difference in the Entrepreneurial Traits among B.Com students based on gender.Objective 3 set for the study "To analyse the Entrepreneurial Traits among B.Com students based on gender" was based on the hypothesis 3 which states that "There is no significant difference in the Entrepreneurial traits among B.Com students based on their gender". The conclusion 3 for the above objective is arrived based on the statistical analysis and is supported by the following findings.

Findings 3.1: The obtained mean value of male = 224, female = 222 and standard deviation of male = 23.9, female = 24.2.

Findings 3.2: The obtained t values ($t = 0.49$, $p > .05$) is not significant at .05 level of significance.

Conclusion 4: There exists no significant difference in the Entrepreneurial Traits among B.Com students based on Type of Institution.Objective 4 set for the study "To analyse the Entrepreneurial

Traits among B.Com students based on Type of Institution" was based on the hypothesis 4 which states that "There is no significant difference in the Entrepreneurial traits among B.Com students based on Type of Institution". The conclusion 4 for the above objective is arrived based on the statistical analysis and is supported by the following findings.

Findings 4.1: The obtained mean value for government = 224, aided = 222 and standard deviation for government = 22.49, aided = 25.43

Findings 4.2: The obtained t values ($t = 0.50$, $p > .05$) is not significant at .05 level of significance

Conclusion 5: There is no significant difference in the Entrepreneurial Traits among B.Com students based on Locality.Objective 4 set for the study "To analyse the Entrepreneurial Traits among B.Com students based on Locality" was based on the hypothesis 4 which states that "There is no significant difference in the Entrepreneurial traits among B.Com students based on Locality". The conclusion 4 for the above objective is arrived based on the statistical analysis and is supported by the following findings.

Findings 5.1: The obtained mean value for rural = 224, urban = 222 and standard deviation for rural = 22.42, urban = 25.49

Findings 5.2: The obtained t values ($t = 0.60$, $p > .05$) is not significant at .05 level of significance

TENABILITY OF HYPOTHESIS

- Hypothesis 1 is stated as, "The level of Entrepreneurial Traits among B.Com students is low". Hypothesis 1 is rejected by the support of the findings 1.1 of the study. **So, the Hypothesis 1 is rejected.**
- Hypothesis 2 states, "There is no significant difference in the mean values of the various components of Entrepreneurial traits among B.Com students". Hypothesis 2 is rejected by the support of the findings 2.1 of the study. **So, Hypothesis 2 is rejected.**
- Hypothesis 3 states that, "There is no significant difference in the entrepreneurial traits among B.Com students based on gender". Hypothesis 3 is accepted by the support of the findings 3.1 and 3.2 of the study. **So, Hypothesis 3 is accepted.**
- Hypothesis 4 states that, "There is no significant difference in the entrepreneurial traits among B.Com students based on Type of Institution". Hypothesis 4 is accepted by the support of the findings 4.1 and 4.2 of the study. **So, Hypothesis 4 is accepted.**
- Hypothesis 5 states that, "There is no significant difference in the entrepreneurial traits among B.Com students based on Locality of the Institution". Hypothesis 5 is accepted by the support of the findings 5.1 and 5.2 of the study. **So, Hypothesis 5 is accepted.**

EDUCATIONAL IMPLICATIONS

Effective curricular transactions require clearly defined, authentic, and activity-focused approaches. Traditional sectors of education are changing due to the need for adaptability, autonomy, collaboration, broad knowledgeability, diversified intellect, and new methods. The teacher who is working well and with distinction and professional esteem is a testament to the educational system's underlying strength. Instead of only developing a person who is proficient in a body of knowledge, learning must aim to develop a certain type of person with a certain disposition and orientation to the world. Curriculum and assessment would need to transition from fragments of study to integrated, comprehensive units of study. In this case, choose a learning agenda that emphasises skill-building above knowledge acquisition.

Learning about an idea is different from acting on it. Entrepreneurship is a style of thinking. In order for students to learn to create jobs rather than study to take jobs, the curriculum is designed to inspire them to imagine and learn new business enterprises. However, a large portion of our official education still encourages this way of thinking. The abilities needed to be an entrepreneur can be taught in an interdisciplinary manner, and they can be designed to inspire students to think entrepreneurially and creatively above pressing global concerns.

The present study tried to analyse the entrepreneurial traits among B.Com students. The analysis of data collected shows that most of the B.Com students possess average Entrepreneurial traits. The changed global scenario demands the need to develop Entrepreneurial traits in order to properly train and educate the learners in accordance with the business enterprises. The subjects studied by commerce students at B.Com level included a large number of units to explore entrepreneurial capabilities of students. Thus, the implications emerged out of the study can be summed up as below:

- The study revealed that majority of the students has average level of Entrepreneurial traits. So, steps should be taken for enhancing Entrepreneurial traits of commerce students at B.Com level. It helps to develop the entrepreneurial habit among students and leads the students to run a business properly
- It is clearly evident from the study that the stress management aspects among B.Com students is poor when compared to other aspects. The institution can organize various programmes and activities in order to manage stress among students.
- The study also reveals that the students need to improve their entrepreneurial traits in order to meet the emerging demands of

economy. So the teachers need to give proper assistance and guidance to the students to improve their entrepreneurial traits.

- The study helps to identify the various entrepreneurial trait component that a student possesses. Therefore, developing educational activities to foster these traits helps students to achieve a successful career growth.
- The integration of theory and practice in commerce education is essential in the twenty-first century. Therefore, developing educational activities to foster entrepreneurial attributes helps students become more creative, self-assured, and socially responsible, which is beneficial in both the personal and societal spheres of daily life.
- The study helps to identify the students with low entrepreneurial traits. Therefore, the school should create situations to encourage the entrepreneurial traits through creative thinking, guidance and counselling, rational thinking and techniques used in daily activities.

RECOMMENDATIONS OF THE STUDY

1. Students can be given the chance to develop these entrepreneurial traits by modifying the curriculum and putting real initiative into action. It is important to focus on developing a learning environment where these abilities are nurtured and developed.
2. The Indian government has made an effort to provide youth with professional and technical education. However, the majority of students are being encouraged to pursue careers rather than starting their own businesses. The kids undoubtedly possess the necessary skills, but they are not likely to choose entrepreneurship as a career unless they are encouraged to do so.
3. Along with their studies, students might be encouraged to engage in small-scale self-employment endeavours, and extra credit may be granted based on how well they accomplish. And also, to foster an entrepreneurial culture inside the Institution, diploma courses on "Entrepreneurial Activities" may be made available.
4. To gauge the degree of entrepreneurial qualities among the students, colleges should establish a separate entrepreneurial cell with trained staff. The colleges may include a separate question regarding future interests on their application form. Specialized curricula and programmes could then be created. Since universities use a semester system, they can provide entrepreneurship courses in the fifth semester to raise awareness of the subject among the students. Visits to nearby industries and a series of lectures by business leaders, marketing specialists, and public officials can

accomplish this. Specific tasks may be completed during the sixth semester. After the course is through, those who want to start their own firm could receive all the start – up assistance they need.

5. Links with other public and private entrepreneurial centres that are prepared to offer internal or joint entrepreneurial training and education must be created. Similar to this, holding regular student-staff forums and colloquia with successful businessmen and entrepreneurs can aid in supplying venues for useful experience sharing and idea sharing. Industry academia collaboration and internship practices need to be strengthened.
6. Educational administrators should organize training programmes, workshops and seminars for the teachers on entrepreneurship education. Educational administrators should also ensure that entrepreneurial education should be made a part of the curriculum for all levels of education so that the concept of entrepreneurship can be strengthened among youth. Entrepreneurship education should also occupy an important place in pre-service training programmes such as B. Ed and D. El. Ed so as to provide necessary skills and knowledge to the future teachers.
7. Teachers and the school authorities should continuously encourage and motivate the students to achieve a successful entrepreneurial career among students by making an awareness on the importance of entrepreneurship, the schemes and policies of government to support entrepreneurs etc., so that they may get an adequate knowledge regarding the benefits of becoming an entrepreneur.
8. All first-generation/new entrepreneurs should be identified by the teachers, and they should receive professional/technical training in entrepreneurship. To prepare entrepreneurs, there is a need for a counselling centre made up of business professionals and educators who work in tandem with educational institutions and businesses.
9. Special consideration must be given to entrepreneurial education. The colleges themselves ought to be entrepreneurial, especially in their interactions with businesses and governmental organisations. Additionally, institutions must view themselves as participants in a market where possibilities come and go and where decisions carry risk. These partnerships must be founded on exchange rather than charity.

SUGGESTIONS FOR FURTHER STUDY

Keeping in mind the limited scope of the present study, further studies are suggested on the following related aspects of entrepreneurial traits among B.Com students in particular and the general population at large:

1. The present study is confined only to B.Com students. It can be studied in any level education.
2. Further studies can also be carried out by developing some learning packages to enhance entrepreneurial traits among students.
3. A study may also be conducted on the current syllabus for entrepreneurship in B.Com level and its effectiveness in developing entrepreneurial mindset among student community
4. Studies can also be undertaken to study the role of Government and NGOs in enhancing entrepreneurial traits among students
5. A study may also be conducted to analyse the entrepreneurial traits among socially and economically backward communities.
6. The present study conducted only in two districts namely Idukki and Kottayam. The study may be extended to other districts of Kerala in context of present alarming Brain-drain.

CONCLUSION

The sector of education needs a suitable curriculum to meet the demands of the pupils because there are new needs. Today, most students pursue higher education in order to find employment or become financially independent. The rush for work would be eliminated if education could be provided with an entrepreneurial orientation because students would pursue careers in self-help. Such a choice would benefit the family and, in turn, society. Additionally, the results of this research have significant ramifications for all parties involved in entrepreneurship education and business development. It is thought that reasonable approaches should be taken to the entrepreneurial traits, which appear to be underdeveloped. All of these traits—initiative, commitment to a work agreement, systematic planning, and risk-taking capacity—need to be fostered and nurtured. Students might be given the chance to acquire these skills by modifying courses and putting practical initiatives into place. Therefore, emphasis should be placed on developing a learning environment where these talents are encouraged and advanced. If the above-mentioned recommendations are implemented, India would soon become an economic superpower.

Appendices

APPENDIX 1: PERSONAL INFORMATION SCHEDULE

MAHATMA GANDHI UNIVERSITY
SCHOOL OF PEDAGOGICAL SCIENCES

Dr. Ismail Thamarasseri (Research Supervisor)

Parvathy Madhusoodhanan (Researcher)

Analysis of Entrepreneurial Traits among B. Com Students

Dear student, I am an M.Ed. student of School of Pedagogical Sciences, Mahatma Gandhi University. This survey is the part of my research studies. I request you to furnish your responses in the following statements. There are five responses given to each statement; 'Always', 'Often', 'Sometimes', 'Rarely', 'Never'. Please carefully read each statement and give your responses by using a tick (✓) mark. I humbly request you to go through the questions carefully ad mark your responses in the space provided. I assure that the information furnished by you will be used solely for research purpose. I express my sincere gratitude for your time.

Personal Details

Name of the student :

Gender : Male☐ Female☐ LGBT☐

Name of the College :

Locality of the College : Urban☐ Rural☐

Type of Institution : Government☐ Govt. Aided☐

APPENDIX 2: ENTREPRENEURIAL TRAIT ASSESSMENT SCALE (DRAFT)

Sl. No.	Dimensions/Statements	Always	Often	Sometimes	Rarely	Never
	A. Conceptual Aspect					
1.	I easily identify problems of a complex situation					
2.	I clarify the nature of the problem before I decide on the action					
3.	It is difficult for me to accept the way in which others solve a problem					
4.	I can find multiple solution to a problem					
5.	I find solution to a problem much faster than others					
6.	It is necessary to have a back-up plan in case the first option does not work					
	B. Technical Aspect					
7.	I constantly follow latest technology					
8.	It is easy for me to use various gadgets					
9.	I am willing to learn new techniques					
10.	I always buy new gadgets					
11.	I frequently participate in technical workshops					
12.	It is difficult for me to deal with new technologies					
	C. Human Relation Aspect					
13.	I easily interact with others					
14.	I can maintain a good relation with others					
15.	It is difficult for me to interact with new people					
16.	I am interested in making new friends					
17.	I face difficulty while working with a team					
18.	I value relationships and professional networks					
	D. Communication Aspect					
19.	I speak confidentially in front of an audience					
20.	I easily get distracted during conversation					
21.	I can draft a corporate letter without errors					
22.	I listen to others carefully					

(Contd...)

Sl. No.	Dimensions/Statements	Always	Often	Sometimes	Rarely	Never
23.	I make my point using simple words that can be understood by all					
24.	I easily learn new languages					
	E. Decision – Making Aspect					
25.	I panic when a problematic situation arises in my life					
26.	I analyse the various aspects of a problem					
27.	I can make quick decisions within a limited period of time					
28.	I often seek the help of others while making crucial decisions					
29	My decisions are correct					
30.	I can choose the wise from the worse					
	F. Managerial Aspect					
31.	I initiate discussion with my peers					
32.	I easily manage all kind of situations					
33.	I am good at giving proper guidance and direction to others					
34.	I am open to the ideas of others					
35.	I accept responsibility for my mistakes					
36.	I refuse to cooperate with my team members					
	G. Time Management Aspect					
37.	I am punctual in my works					
38.	I arrange my activities based on their urgency					
39.	I wait for the deadline to complete my works					
40.	I keep a 'time table' and 'things-to-do' list					
41.	I seek the help of others to prevent project delays					
	H. Stress Management Aspect					
42.	I can adapt to changing circumstances					

(Contd...)

Sl. No.	Dimensions/Statements	Always	Often	Sometimes	Rarely	Never
43.	I easily get frustrated when difficulties arise					
44.	I can manage multi-tasking					
45.	I can control my emotions					
46.	I keep myself calm when faced with difficulties					
47.	I skip difficult situations					
	I. Personality & Individual Aspect					
48.	I am amiable and outgoing					
49.	My attitude is positive when I experience failure					
50.	I plan my day-to-day activities well ahead of time					
51.	I feel difficult to arrange my things in an organised manner					
52.	I follow and uphold the principles of my college/university					
53.	I always run away from complex situations					
	J. Pioneering Skill/Risk taking Aspect					
54.	I keep myself updated of the latest trends					
55.	When doing a task, I often devise new ways to complete it faster and better					
56.	I often face difficulty in exploring innovative practices in life					
57.	When assigned with project works, I make sure to choose the latest and significant topics					
58.	I frequently search for new opportunities					
59.	It is interested for me to take challenges in life					
	K. Unification & Organization Aspect					
60.	I get frustrated when someone motivates me					
61.	It is difficult for me to make a proper schedule and plan for everything					
62.	I can motivate others to work for a common goal					
63.	I can communicate ideas to persuade and convince others					

(Contd...)

Sl. No.	Dimensions/Statements	Always	Often	Sometimes	Rarely	Never
64.	I work with different clubs and associations of my college					
65.	I take lead to organise events in my college					
	L. Computer Knowledge Aspect					
66.	I have enough knowledge to use a computer					
67.	It is a difficult task for me to study various computer programmes					
68.	I am able to use various software					
69.	I quickly learn to use a new software					
70.	I am interested in attending various ICT workshops					

APPENDIX 3: ENTREPRENEURIAL TRAIT ASSESSMENT SCALE (FINAL)

Sl. No.	Dimensions/Statements	Always	Often	Sometimes	Rarely	Never
	A. Conceptual Aspect					
1.	I easily identify problems of a complex situation					
2.	I clarify the nature of the problem before I decide on the action					
3.	It is difficult for me to accept the way in which others solve a problem					
4.	I find solution to a problem much faster than others					
5.	It is necessary to have a back-up plan in case the first option does not work					
	B. Technical Aspect					
6.	I constantly follow latest technology					
7.	It is easy for me to use various gadgets					
8.	I am willing to learn new techniques					
9.	I frequently participate in technical workshops					
10.	It is difficult for me to deal with new technologies					
	C. Human Relation Aspect					
11.	I easily interact with others					
12.	I can maintain a good relation with others					
13.	I am interested in making new friends					
14.	I face difficulty while working with a team					
15.	I value relationships and professional networks					
	D. Communication Aspect					
16.	I speak confidentially in front of an audience					
17.	I easily get distracted during conversation					
18.	I can draft a corporate letter without errors					
19.	I listen to others carefully					
20.	I make my point using simple words that can be understood by all					

(Contd...)

Sl. No.	Dimensions/Statements	Always	Often	Sometimes	Rarely	Never
	E. Decision – Making Aspect					
21.	I panic when a problematic situation arises in my life					
22.	I analyse the various aspects of a problem					
23.	I can make quick decisions within a limited period of time					
24.	I often seek the help of others while making crucial decisions					
25.	I can choose the wise from the worse					
	F. Managerial Aspect					
26.	I initiate discussion with my peers					
27.	I am good at giving proper guidance and direction to others					
28.	I am open to the ideas of others					
29.	I accept responsibility for my mistakes					
30.	I refuse to cooperate with my team members					
	G. Time Management Aspect					
31.	I am punctual in my works					
32.	I arrange my activities based on their urgency					
33.	I wait for the deadline to complete my works					
34.	I keep a 'time table' and 'things-to-do' list					
35.	I seek the help of others to prevent project delays					
	H. Stress Management Aspect					
36.	I can adapt to changing circumstances					
37.	I easily get frustrated when difficulties arise					
38.	I can manage multi-tasking					
39.	I can control my emotions					
40.	I keep myself calm when faced with difficulties					

(Contd...)

Sl. No.	Dimensions/Statements	Always	Often	Sometimes	Rarely	Never
	I. Personality & Individual Aspect					
41.	I am amiable and outgoing					
42.	My attitude is positive when I experience failure					
43.	I plan my day-to-day activities well ahead of time					
44.	I feel difficult to arrange my things in an organised manner					
45.	I follow and uphold the principles of my college/university					
	J. Pioneering Skill/Risk taking Aspect					
46.	I keep myself updated of the latest trends					
47.	When doing a task, I often devise new ways to complete it faster and better					
48.	I often face difficulty in exploring innovative practices in life					
49.	When assigned with project works, I make sure to choose the latest and significant topics					
50.	I frequently search for new opportunities					
	K. Unification & Organization Aspect					
51.	It is difficult for me to make a proper schedule and plan for everything					
52.	I can motivate others to work for a common goal					
53.	I can communicate ideas to persuade and convince others					
54.	I work with different clubs and associations of my college					
55.	I take lead to organise events in my college					
	L. Computer Knowledge Aspect					
56.	I have enough knowledge to use a computer					
57.	It is a difficult task for me to study various computer programmes					
58.	I am able to use various software					
59.	I quickly learn to use a new software					
60.	I am interested in attending various ICT workshops					

Bibliography

1. Abraham, M.M. (2010). *Entrepreneurship Development & Project management (1st ed.).* Prakash publications.
2. Adeyamo, A.S. (2009). Understanding and Acquisition of Entrepreneurial Skills: A Pedagogical Re-orientation for Classroom Teacher in Science Education. *Journal of Turkish Science Education,* 6(3), 57-65.
3. Ahmed, U., Pahi, M.H., Mozammel, S., & Umrani, W.A. (2018). Entrepreneurial Intentions amongst Female Students: Test of a Moderated Model in an Emerging Economy. *The Turkish online Journal of Design, Art and Communication,* 3080-3091. https://www. researchgate. net/publication/ 328265841 _Entrepreneurial _Intentions_ Amongst_ Female _Students _Test _of_ a_ Moderated _Model_ in_ an_ Emerging _Economy
4. Ali, A., Topping, K.J., & Tariq, H.R. (2011). Entrepreneurial Attitudes among Potential Entrepreneurs. *Pakistan Journal of Commerce, Social Science,* 5(1), 12-46. http://www.jespk.net/publications/43.pdf
5. Amubode, A.A., & Goriola, O.R. (2015). Assessment of Entrepreneurial Traits among Undergraduate Students of Clothing, Textile and Interior Decoration. *International Journal of Marketing Studies,* 7(4). https://doi.org/10.5539/ijms.v7n4p94
6. Angelica, M., & Ramos. (2014). Entrepreneurial Intentions among Business Students in Batangas State University. *Asia Pacific Journal of Multidisciplinary Research,* 2(4).
7. Antony, V.R. (2014). *Effectiveness of Jurisprudential Inquiry Model on Academic Performance, Entrepreneurial Skills and Social Competence among Commerce students at Higher secondary level* [Unpublished doctoral dissertation]. Mahatma Gandhi University.
8. Ashoka, M.L., & Abhirami, M. (2018). A Study on the Performance Evaluation of Entrepreneurial Assistance schemes of SIDBI to MSMEs in Karnataka. *Review of Research,* 7(12). http://oldror.lbp.world/UploadedData/5841.pdf

9. Audet, J. (2008). Two Pedagogical Approaches to Entrepreneurship Education using an Intention - based Model of Venture Creation. *Journal of Management Studies*, 34(6), 895-920.
10. Awang, A., Amran, S., Nor, M.N., Ibrahim, I.I., & Razali, M.F. (2016). Individual Entrepreneurial Orientation Impact on Entrepreneurial Intention: Intervening Effect of PBC and Subjective Norm. *Journal of Entrepreneurship, Business and Economics*, 4(2), 94-99.
11. Bashir, H.A. (2016). The Role of Innovative Entrepreneurship in Economic Development: A Study of G20 Countries. *Management Studies and Economic Systems*, 3(2), 91-100. https://doi.org/10.12816/0037559
12. Baum, J.R., & Locke, E.A. (2004). The Relationship of Entrepreneurial Traits, Skill, and Motivation to Subsequent Venture Growth. *Journal of Applied Psychology*, 89(4), 587-598. https://doi.org/10.1037/0021-9010.89.4.587
13. Begam, M., Abdul, K., & Salim. (2012). Factors Affecting Entrepreneurial Intentions among Professional College Students, Academy of Management Journal. *Academy of Management Journal*, 23(3).
14. Best, J.W., & Kahn, V.J. (1997). *Research in Education*. Prentice - Hall India.
15. Best, J.W., & Kahn, V.J. (2005). *Research in Education*. Prentice - Hall India.
16. Best, J.W., & Kahn, V.J. (2006). *Research in Education*. Prentice - Hall India.
17. Bhandari, N.C. (2006). Intention for Entrepreneurship among Students in India. *The Journal of Entrepreneurship*, 15(2), 169-179. https://doi.org/10.1177/097135570601500204
18. Bhuyan, M. (2021). *Entrepreneurial Intent Assessment among University Students in Uttarakhand Region* [Doctoral dissertation]. http://hdl.handle.net/10603/355872
19. Blasco, M., Guijarro, A., & Lema, D. (2016). Entrepreneurial Skills and Socio-cultural Factors: An Empirical Analysis in Secondary Education Students. *Education + Training*, 58(7/8). https://doi.org/10.1108/et-06-2015-0054
20. Botha, M., Nieman, G., & Vuuren, J. (2006). Enhancing Female Entrepreneurship by Enabling Access to Skills. *The International Entrepreneurship and Management Journal*, 2(4), 479-493. https://doi.org/10.1007/s11365-006-0011-2
21. Chandra, S.S., & Sharma (2004). *Research in Education*. Atlantic Publishers and Distributers.
22. Chaudhari, T. (2013). A Study of Entrepreneurial Attitude among Post Graduate Students. *Research Journal of Commerce and Behavioural Science*, 2(6), 12-17.

23. Chawala, S.A., & Butare, A. (2005). Developing Entrepreneurial Competencies amongst Rwandan Youth. *Indian Marketing Studies Journal*, 9(1).

24. Collins, L., Hannon, P.D., & Smith, A. (2006). Enacting Entrepreneurial Intent: The Gaps between Student needs and Higher Education Capability. *Education + Training*, 46(8/9), 454-463. https://doi.org/10.1108/00400910410569579

25. Dhaliwal, A. (2016). Role of Entrepreneurship in Economic Development. *International Journal of scientific research and management*. https://doi.org/10.18535/ijsrm/v4i6.08

26. Edwards, L., & Muir, E.J. (2012). Evaluating Enterprise Education: Why do it? *Education + Training, 54*(4), 278-290. https://doi.org/10.1108/00400911211236136

27. Gondim, S.M., & Mutti, C. (2011). Affections in Learning Situations: A Study of an Entrepreneurship Skills Development Course. *Journal of Workplace Learning*, 23(3), 195-208. https://doi.org/10.1108/13665621111117224

28. Gürol, Y., & Atsan, N. (2006). Entrepreneurial Characteristics amongst University Students. *Education + Training, 48*(1), 25-38. https://doi.org/10.1108/00400910610645716

29. Guthrie, G. (2010). *Basic Research methods: An Entry to Social Science Research*. SAGE Publishing India.

30. Hägg, G., & Kurczewska, A. (2021). *Entrepreneurship Education: Scholarly Progress and Future Challenges*. Routledge. https://www.taylorfrancis.com/books/oa-mono/10.4324/9781003194972/entrepreneurship-education-gustav-h%C3%A4gg-agnieszka-kurczewska

31. Hattab, H.W. (2014). Impact of Entrepreneurship Education on Entrepreneurial Intentions of University Students in Egypt. *The Journal of Entrepreneurship*, 23(1), 1-18. https://doi.org/10.1177/0971355713513346

32. Herath, H., & Amarawansha, T. (2018). Students Career Attitudes towards Entrepreneurship. *International Journal of Research and Innovation in Social Science*, 2(6), 14-18.

33. Hmedat, D.W., Ali, M., & Muthuraman, D.B. (2017). A Study on Entrepreneurial Initiatives among Mba Students in Sultanate of Oman. *International Journal of Management, Innovation & Entrepreneurial Research*, 3(2), 78-91. https://doi.org/10.18510/ijmier.2017.324

34. Ilhan Ertuna, Z., & Gurel, E. (2011). The Moderating Role of Higher Education on Entrepreneurship. *Education + Training, 53*(5), 387-402. https://doi.org/10.1108/00400911111147703

35. Ilyas, T.M. (2010). Entrepreneur Generation and Entrepreneurial Success - An Empirical Study. *SEDME (Small Enterprises Development, Management & Extension Journal): A Worldwide Window on MSME Studies*, 37(1), 19-26. https://doi.org/10.1177/0970846420100102
36. Iroegbu, V.I. (2017). The Attitudes of Higher Degree Students to Entrepreneurial Skills Training in Early Childhood Education. *Journal of Education and Human Development*, 6(2). https://doi.org/10.15640/jehd.v6n1a18
37. Isah, U.G., & Hashim, N. (2018). The Influence of Entrepreneurial Competencies on Entrepreneurial Career Option among Polytechnic Students in Nigeria. *European Journal of Business and Management, 10*(3).
38. Jayaprakash, K. (2015). *Effectiveness of ISMAN Instructional Design Model for Facilitating Skill of Entrepreneurship and Creative thinking among Commerce Students at Higher Secondary School Level* [Unpublished master's Thesis]. Mahatma Gandhi University.
39. Jesselyn, M., & Mitchell, B. (2006). Entrepreneurship Education in South Africa: A Nationwide Survey. *Education + Training*, 48(5), 348-359.
40. Jusoh, R., Ziyae, B., Asimiran, S., & Kadir, S.A. (2011). Entrepreneur Training needs Analysis: Implications on the Entrepreneurial Skills needed for Successful Entrepreneurs. *International Business & Economics Research Journal (IBER)*, 10(1). https://doi.org/10.19030/iber.v10i1.933
41. Karim, S., & Venkataiah, C. (2016). A Comparative Study on Attitude towards Entrepreneurship among MBA and other Students. *International Journal of Science Technology and Management*, 5(1), 249-261. http://data.conferenceworld.in/SVCET/P249-261.pdf
42. Khursheed, A. (2017). Entrepreneurial Perceptions of Students of University of Central Punjab, Lahore and also finding the Hindrances they Perceive. *Journal of Business & Financial Affairs, 06*(02). https://doi.org/10.4172/2167-0234.1000263
43. Korhonen, M., Komulainen, K., & Räty, H. (2012). "Not Everyone is cut out to be the Entrepreneur Type": How Finnish School Teachers Construct the meaning of Entrepreneurship Education and the Related Abilities of the Pupils. *Scandinavian Journal of Educational Research*, 56(1), 1-19. https://doi.org/10.1080/00313831.2011.567393
44. Krishna, D. (2012). *Effectiveness of Multimedia Learning Package based on VARK Model for Enhancing Decision making and Entrepreneurial Traits among Commerce Students at Higher Secondary Level* [Unpublished Master's Thesis]. Mahatma Gandhi University.
45. Kumar, A. (2010). Entrepreneurs in Small Scale Sector: A Study of Infrastructural Barriers. *SEDME (Small Enterprises Development,*

Management & Extension Journal): A Worldwide Window on MSME Studies, 37(4), 19-32. https://doi.org/10.1177/0970846420100402

46. Kumar, E.A. (2015). *A Study on Entrepreneurial Traits among Students of Arts and Science Colleges in Thoothukudi District* [Unpublished doctoral dissertation].
47. Küttim, M., Kallaste, M., Venesaar, U., & Kiis, A. (2014). Entrepreneurship Education at University Level and Students' Entrepreneurial Intentions. *Procedia - Social and Behavioral Sciences,* 110, 658-668. https://doi.org/10.1016/j.sbspro.2013.12.910.
48. Lans, T., Blok, V., & Wesselink, R. (2014). Learning Apart and together: Towards an Integrated Competence Framework for Sustainable Entrepreneurship in Higher Education. *Journal of Cleaner Production,* 62, 37-47. https://doi.org/10.1016/j.jclepro.2013.03.036
49. Lee, Y.S. (2016). Entrepreneurship, Small Businesses and Economic Growth in Cities. *Journal of Economic Geography,* lbw021. https://doi.org/10.1093/jeg/lbw021
50. Lokesh, K. (2003). *Methodology of Educational Research* (5th ed.). Vikas Publishing House.
51. Maalu, K.J., Nzuve, M.S., & Magutu, O.P. (2010). A Survey of Personal Goals and Perception of Entrepreneurial Ability among Students at the School of Business. *University of Nairobi, Management,* 35(1), 24-33.
52. Majeed, S. (2016). Awareness and Inclination towards Entrepreneurship among College Students of Kashmir. *IRA-International Journal of Management & Social Sciences (ISSN 2455-2267), 3*(2). https://doi.org/10.21013/jmss.v3.n2.p7
53. Mbanefo, M.C., & Ebokab, O.C. (2017). Acquisition of Innovative and Entrepreneurial Skills in basic Science Education for Job Creation in Nigeria. *Science Education International,* 28(3), 207-213. https://doi.org/10.33828/sei.v28.i3.4
54. Mclaughlin, E.B. (2010). The Role of Emotional Intelligence and Self-efficacy in Developing Entrepreneurial Career Intentions. *Academy of Management Proceedings,* 2010(1), 1-5. https://doi.org/10.5465/ambpp.2010.54500673
55. Meredith, G.G., Nelson, R.E., & Neck, P.A., (1982). *The Practice of Entrepreneurship.* Dialogue Publications.
56. Mertens, D.M. (2010). *Transformative Research and Evaluation.* Guilford Press.
57. Muhammad, Z. (2013). Entrepreneurial Characteristics among University Students: Implications for Entrepreneurship Education and Training in Pakistan. *African Journal of Business Management,* 7(39).

58. Naimatullah, S., & Bahadur, A. (2013). Investigating Attitudes and Intentions among Potential Entrepreneurs of a Developing Country: A Coceptual Approach. *International Conference on Humanities, Economics and Geography.*

59. Nisha, A. (2015). *Entrepreneurial Intensions, School of Management, Faculty of Engineering and Technology* [Doctoral dissertation]. http:// hdl.handle.net/ 10603/50949.

60. Nkiruka, E., Eskay, M., Joy, A., & Ikwumelu. (2013). Preliminary Identification of Performance – Oriented Competences for Undergraduates' Entrepreneurial Education via Information Communication Technology (ICT) for Wealth Creation in Enugu State, Nigeria, *International Journal of Computer Science,* 10(5).

61. Nuradhi, M., & Kristanti, L. (2021). Opportunity Recognition: Gender and Family Business Background Comparison. International Journal of Family Business Practices, 3(2), 18-32.

62. Omidi Najafabadi, M., Zamani, M., & Mirdamadi, M. (2016). Designing a Model for Entrepreneurial Intentions of Agricultural Students. *Journal of Education for Business,* 91(6), 338-346. https://doi.org/10.1080/ 08832323.2016.1218318

63. Osakede, U.A., Lawanson, A.O., & Sobowale, D.A. (2017). Entrepreneurial Interest and Academic Performance in Nigeria: Evidence from Undergraduate Students in the University of Ibadan. *Journal of Innovation and Entrepreneurship,* 6(1). https://doi.org/10.1186/ s13731-017-0079-7

64. Politis, D. (2017). The Process of Entrepreneurial Learning: A Conceptual Framework. *Entrepreneurship Theory and Practice,* 29(4), 399-424. https:/ /doi.org/10.1111/j.1540-6520.2005.00091.x

65. Pulka, B.M., Aminu, A.A., & Rikwentishe, R. (2015). The Effects of Entrepreneurship Education on University Students - Attitude and Entrepreneurial Intention. *European Journal of Business and Management,* 7(20).

66. Rahmawati, F., Hasyyati, A., & Yusran, H.L. (2012). The Obstacles to be Young Entrepreneur. *The 2012 International Conference on Business and Management,* 6(2), 462-472.

67. Rathna, C., Badrinath, V., & Anushan, S.C. (2016). A Study on Entrepreneurial Motivation and Challenges Faced by Women Entrepreneurs in Thanjavur District. *Indian Journal of Science and Technology,* 9(27). https://doi.org/10.17485/ijst/2016/v9i27/97594

68. Raza, S., & Nizamuddin, F. (2008). Factors Affecting Entrepreneurship Intention Levels of Graduating Students in Pakistan. *Journal of Management,* 35(2), 139-161.

69. Rengamani, J., & Ramachandran, S. (2015). A Study on the Entrepreneurial Skills among Students in Chennai. *International Journal of Advanced Research in Management*, 6(3), 36-44.

70. Renugadevi, S., & Antony, B. (2016). Entrepreneurial Traits among College Students in Madurai City. *International Journal of Management and Development Studies*, 5(1), 10-15.

71. Reyad, S.M., Badawi, S.S., & Hamdan, A. M. (2018). Entrepreneurship and Accounting Students' Career in the Arab Region: Conceptual Perspective. *The Journal of Developing Areas*, 52(4), 283-288. https://doi.org/10.1353/jda.2018.0065

72. Sajjad, A.M. (2020). *Effectiveness of Entrepreneurship Skill Development Programme Conducted by Micro Small Medium Enterprises Development Institute Kerala* [Doctoral dissertation]. http://14.139.116.20:8080/jspui/handle/10603/344684

73. Sankar, & Sutha, I. (2016). College Student Mind-set and Intentions toward Entrepreneurship in Chennai City. *International Journal of Research -granthaalayah*, 4(8(SE)), 36-39. https://doi.org/10.29121/granthaalayah.v4.i8(se).2016.2584

74. Satheesh, A. (2019). *Effectiveness of Game based Learning Strategy of Entrepreneurship Ability and Achievement in Commerce of Vocational Higher Secondary School Students* [Unpublished master's thesis]. Mahatma Gandhi University.

75. Schwarz, E.J., Wdowiak, M.A., Almer Jarz, D.A., & Breitenecker, R.J. (2009). The Effects of Attitudes and Perceived Environment Conditions on Students' Entrepreneurial Intent. *Education + Training*, *51*(4), 272-291. https://doi.org/10.1108/00400910910964566

76. Setiadi, N.J., & Puspitasari, D.M. (2014). Empirical Study of Entrepreneurial Attitudes and Intentions among Indonesian Business Students. *DLSL Journal of Management*, *1*(1).

77. Sidi Ali, R. (2018). Feminist Theory and its Influence on Female Entrepreneur's Growth Intentions. *International Journal of Innovation and Economic Development*, 4(3), 20-32. https://doi.org/10.18775/ijied.1849-7551-7020.2015.43.2003

78. Soleimanpour, M.R., Hosseini, S.J.F., & Farzam, M. (2014). *Study of the Relationship between Entrepreneurial Characteristics and Students' Academic Achievement* [Doctoral dissertation]. https://www.cibtech.org/sp.ed/jls/2014/03/JLS-141-S3-165-Reza-Study-Achievement.pdf

79. Stephen, D., & Antony, B. (2017). Attitude towards Entrepreneurship among the Students of Business Studies. *International Journal of Human Resource, Management and Research*, 7(1).

80. Sudarwati, N. (2018). Compiling Integrated Entrepreneurship module by using Design-based Research Approach to Improve Students' Entrepreneurial Skill. *Journal of Sustainable Development*, 11(1), 83. https://doi.org/10.5539/jsd.v11n1p83

81. Sujatha, S. (2019). *Relationship Among Entrepreneurial Skills, Intelligence and Vocational Aspirations of Commerce Students at Undergraduate Level* [Unpublished doctoral dissertation]. Mahatma Gandhi University.

82. Sutanto, E.M., & Eliyana, A. (2014). *The Study of Entrepreneurial Characteristics with Achievement Motivation and Attitude as the Antecedent Variables* [Doctoral dissertation]. https://www.proquest.com/openview/850fa606dcee26efa6483e7febc39620/1?pq-origsite=gscholar&cbl=556342

83. Tamizharasi, G., & Panchanatham, N. (2010). An Empirical Study of Demographic Variables on Entrepreneurial Attitudes. *International Journal of Trade, Economics and Finance*, 1(2), 215-220. https://doi.org/10.7763/ijtef.2010.v1.40

84. Thamarasseri, I. (2007). *Education in the Emerging Indian Society*. Kanishka Publishers.

85. Udoukpong, E.B., Emah, I.E., & Umoren, E.S. (2012). Student Attitudes, Parental Influence and Career Aspirations in Academic Achievement in Entrepreneurial Curricuum. *Academic Research International*, 2(1), 21-52. http://www.savap.org.pk/journals/ARint./Vol.2(1)/2012(21-52).pdf

86. Varalakshmi, C., Srivani, N., & Srinivasa Rao, P. (2019). An Empirical Study on Youth Perception towards Entrepreneurship with Reference to Vijayawada city. *International Journal of Advanced Research*, 7(1), 12-22. https://doi.org/10.21474/ijar01/8291

87. Varghese, A.R. (2009). *Effectiveness of Creative Problem-solving Strategy for Enhancing Entrepreneurial Skills among Commerce Students at Higher Secondary Level* [Master's Thesis]. Mahatma Gandhi University.

88. Vasant, D. (2012). *Entrepreneurship and Management of Small and Medium Enterprises* (2nd ed.). Himalaya Publishing House.

89. Viji, S., & Sharma, P. (2013). Does Entrepreneurial Education Enhance the Entrepreneurial Drive of Business Students. *The IUP Journal of Entrepreneurship Development*, 10(2), 65-82.

90. Vorley, T., & Williams, N. (2016). Not just Dialling it in. *Education + Training*, *58*(1), 45-60. https://doi.org/10.1108/et-01-2015-0010

91. Wilson, F., Kickul, J., & Marlino, D. (2007). Gender, Entrepreneurial Self-efficacy, and Entrepreneurial Career Intentions: Implications for Entrepreneurship Education. *Entrepreneurship Theory and Practice*, 31(3), 387-406. https://doi.org/10.1111/j.1540-6520.2007.00179.x

92. Yanya, M., Hakim, R., & Razak, N.A. (2013). Does Entrepreneurship bring an Equal Society and Alleviate Poverty? Evidence from Thailand. *Procedia - Social and Behavioral Sciences*, 91, 331-340. https://doi.org/10.1016/j.sbspro.2013.08.430
93. Yeigh, T., Lynch, D., Fradale, P., Lawless, E., Turner, D., & Willis, R. (2021). *Improving Schools with Blended Learning: How to make Technology Work in the Modern Classroom*. Routledge.
94. Zaidatol, A.L., & Abdullah, S. (2009). Exploring the Entrepreneurial mindset of Students: Implication for Improvement of Entrepreneurial Learning at University. *The Journal of International Social Research*, 21(8), 340-343.
95. Zhao, H., Seibert, S.E., & Hills, G. E. (2005). The Mediating Role of Self-efficacy in the Development of Entrepreneurial Intentions. Journal of Applied Psychology, 90, 1265-1272.

Index

A

Adiseshiah Committee, 2

Analysis and interpretation of data, 89-100

- analysis of data, 90
- entrepreneurial traits among B.Com students, 91
  - based on its components, 93-95
  - on the basis of
    - gender, 95-96
    - locality, 99-100
    - type of institution, 96-98
- hypotheses, 90
- introduction, 89-91
- level of entrepreneurial traits, 92-93

Atal Incubation Centres (AICs), 36

Atal Innovation Mission (AIM), 36

Atal Tinkering Labs (ATL), 36

B

Biotechnology Industry Research Assistance Council, 37

C

Commerce Education, 4, 6

Communication Skills, 21

Curriculum, 2, 4

D

Department of Science and Technology, 37

Digital Age, 8

Digital India, 37

E

Education, 1

Empathy, 21

Entrepreneur, 6, 7, 11, 15

- characteristics, 16
- functions of, 17-19
- goal setter, 17
- high energy level, 17
- initiative, 17
- long term involvement, 17
- moderate risk taker, 17
- motivator, 17
- persistent problem solver, 17
- self-confidence, 17
- time management, 25-26

Entrepreneurship

- concept of, 11
- education, 3, 13
- history of, 7-8
- social, 8, 10

Entrepreneurship education, 3, 13

- history of, 9-13
- importance of, 34

F

Findings, Suggestions and Conclusion, 101-107

- educational implications, 104-105
- findings of the study, 102-103
- introduction, 101
- methodology in brief, 101-102
- recommendations, 105-106
- study in retrospect, 101

suggestions, 108-109
tenability of hypotheses, 103

G

Globalization, 8, 9
Government of India, 34

I

Industrial Revolution, 7
Institutions set up by Central Government, 38-42
All India Small Scale Industries Board, 39
Centre for Entrepreneurial Development, 41
Entrepreneurship Development Institute of India, 39
Indian Institute of Entrepreneurship, 41
Indian Investment Centre, 40
Institute for Entrepreneurial Development, 41
Institutions set up at State Level, 42
Khadi and village industries Commission, 40
Management Development Institute, 39
Miscellaneous Organization, 41
National Alliance of Young Entrepreneurs, 41
National Institute of Small Industries Extension Training, 40
National Institution of Entrepreneurship and Small Business Development, 39-40
National Research and Development Corporation, 40
National Small Industries Corporation Ltd., 40
Public sector banks, 42
Risk Capital and Technology Finance Corporation Ltd., 40
Small industries development organization, 38
Technical Consultancy Organization, 41-42

Introduction, 1-47
aims of teaching commerce, 6
characteristics of entrepreneurs, 15-17
communication, 22-23
computer knowledge, 3132
conceptual traits, 19-20
decision-making, 24-25
entrepreneurial competencies, 13-15
entrepreneurial traits, 19
evolution of entrepreneurship, 6-7
functions of an entrepreneur, 1718
history of entrepreneurship, 7
human relation, 21-22
hypotheses of the study, 44
importance of entrepreneurship education, 34
limitations of the study, 40
methodology of the study, 44-45
need and significance of the study, 42-43
objectives of
commerce education, 6
the study, 44
operational definition of key terms, 44
organisation of the report, 46-47
organizational traits, 30-31
other functions, 18-19
personality and individual trait, 27-28
pioneering, 28-29
role and importance of entrepreneur, 32-34
role of government in promoting entrepreneurship, 34
scope of the study, 45-46
statement of the problem, 43
stress management, 26-27
technical traits, 20-21
theoretical overview of the study, 4-5
time management, 25-26
unification and organization, 30
Ishwar Bhai Patel Committee, 2

J

Jan Dhan-Aadhaar-Mobile (JAM), 36

K

Kalam, Dr. A P J Abdul, 1, 3

Kothari Commission (1964-1966), 2

Kunkel, John, 11

L

Liberal education, 5

M

Made in India, 35-36

Methodology, 73-88

collection of data, 85

description of tools and techniques adopted, 78

design of the study, 76

distribution of sample, 77

entrepreneurial traits, 76, 79, 73

assessment scale, 79-82, 83-85

hypotheses of the study, 75

introduction, 73

method adopted for the study, 75-76

objectives, 74

of the study, 75

personal information schedule, 79

pilot study, 79

population, sample and sampling procedure, 76-78

preparation of the

data collection, 85

initial draft, 79

second draft, 79

random sampling technique, 77

reliability of the test, 84

research methodology, 74

sampling is the process, 76

scoring and consolidation of data, 85

scoring procedure, 79-80

standardization procedure, 80-83

statistical techniques used for the study, 85-88

tools of research, 78

validity and reliability, 74

validity of the test, 83-84

Ministry of Skill Development and Entrepreneurship (MSDE), 34

Modi, Narendra, 35

N

National Skill Development Mission, 38

NCF-2005, 3

Networking Skills, 22

P

Pradhan Mantri Kaushal Vikas Yojana, 38

Pradhan Mantri Yuva Yojana (PMYY), 34

R

Review of the related literature, 48-72

advantages, 62

business students, 63

entrepreneurial characteristics of the students, 60

entrepreneurial trait, 62

entrepreneurship education, 60

entrepreneurship profile, 63

ICT and entrepreneurial competences, 62

impact of entrepreneurship, 61

introduction, 48-50

psychological model based on Ajzen's theory of planned behaviour, 63

relationship between entrepreneurial characteristics and students, 60

sustainable entrepreneurs, 61

S

Science for Equity Empowerment and Development, 38

Start-up India, 35

STEM (Science, Technology, Engineering, and Math), 36

Stress Management, 26-27

Support to Training and Employment Programme for Women (STEP), 36

T

Team Building, 21

Trade related Entrepreneurship Assistance and Development, 37

V

Vivekananda, Swami

W

Weber, Max, 11

Women, 35

Working and learning, 2

World War II, 8

❑ ❑ ❑ ❑ ❑ ❑